~

For Hunter,
You're the book I never knew I needed to write, the
missing chapters to my life.
Inspired by you, for you and because of you.

~

~

"Paul's excellent book offers
a valuable and much needed insight into what happens
when things go wrong in pregnancy. The account of a dad
isn't often heard and even more rarely written down. With a
mix of shock, humour and self-depreciation, Paul tells his
story and that of his family in a pacy, hard hitting and
bittersweet way.
This book is a must read for anyone involved in the care of
families going through pregnancy when things get hard,
because ultimately, we need to look beyond the baby to the
whole family."

Marcus Green, CEO
APEC, ACTION ON PRE-ECLAMPSIA

~

CONTENTS

~

CONTENTS

~

CHAPTER ONE

~

Daddy Doubts

I had just returned to the office from an eventful market appraisal, Ashbourne Grove, three-bedroom semi-detached Victorian house, primely located for catchment to the best primary and secondary schools in the area.

"Elderflower and lime cordial?" yes please I replied, "still or sparking", couldn't believe I got a choice but went for sparking, the seller of the property then proceeded to pour sparking water from her fancy new copper tap, the ones that pour instant boiling water, so you don't need a kettle. We sat at the dining table for a chat, having just wiped sick off my shoulder from holding the sellers six-month-old baby whilst she looked for the old details of when she purchased the property. Tears soon rained upon my other shoulder as she explained the reason she was selling the property, was due to her husband's infidelity with the local florist Lily who lived on the neighbouring street. I was tempted to ask if she had anything stronger to put in my drink. If that drama wasn't enough, I almost fell through the bedroom ceiling having felt compelled to go up in the web infested loft so I could see how enormous the space was up there, "largest on the road" apparently", I then had to play hopscotch in the garden as I leaped over carefully positioned dogs mess courtesy of her two Russian terriers.

I then came back to the car to find a parking ticket as I was 3 minutes late, thankfully I won the signed terms of business and received keys to the property. Standard afternoon as an estate agent in leafy Dulwich, sometimes resembling an episode of desperate housewives or Selling Sunset, but without the sun, but at its core is a wonderful family area with vibrant market stalls, coffee shops, independent retailers, community culture and private schools that belong in a Harry Potter film or Downton Abbey. Far away from what I saw growing up on a day-to-day basis and to be honest, aspirational.

Flustered from my elderflower cordial ordeal and filling my work colleagues in on the story over a well-deserved cup of tea, I saw my phone flashing with missed calls from my partner Lauren, followed by a text message that would change my world. 18th May 2019, 2:30pm, "OMG babe, I've just done a test, I'm pregnant". I Froze, "Paul, no way was he shagging the flower girl, what happened next?" my staff wanted the next chapter of the story I was telling them, not knowing I was about to take centre stage in my own award-winning novel. "Someone go Marks and Spencer and get some biscuits, ill finish telling you all shortly", I said "Just need to make a call". I then nervously and excitedly returned the call out the back in the carpark.

I knew I wanted to have the baby, but it wasn't planned, and we had to decide together with the final decision ultimately being with her, you know, a woman's body a woman's choice. I had been disappointed twice before much younger in my late teens and then five years previously and the decision was made that we didn't want to keep the child, her choice. I couldn't accept that decision, though respected it was hers to make, and it ultimately destroyed that relationship, was Lauren going to feel the same? Did she think I would be a good father? I mean, she is younger than me, eight-year age gap, so is she going to feel ready? I nervously called her, and we talked it all through and thankfully she shared my sentiment that no matter what, we wanted to keep baby, it then immediately became real, I was going to be dad!

Feelings of excitement, confidence, joy, love and responsibility were instant, I want to be the perfect dad, I grew up without one. These positive affirmations swiftly provoked thoughts of my childhood and doubt quickly ensued. All the dormant feelings of abandonment, isolation, disappointment, and vulnerabilities came flooding back like a tsunami, I was back to being 6 years old again.

How could I possibly be a good dad? I don't know what that feels or looks like, as I had no one to learn from. The closest and most consistent male role model that looked like me I saw growing up, appeared every Tuesday at 6pm on BBC2. Uncle Phil from The Fresh Prince of Bel Air, a successful black man who looked after and cherished his family providing a platform for them to thrive, that I could one day aspire to be like. Fictional TV story of course, but powerful in showcasing real life Black family dynamics in a positive light that is sadly too infrequently shown. Sir Trevor Macdonald on ITV news at 10pm was another, he was articulate, professional and the main anchor on prime-time British television, inspirational. Though he was also a constant reminder of the overwhelming underrepresentation of black British figures in UK mainstream media for me to aspire to be, that were in positions of influence and status that could empower others to follow a similar road. So much so, that I had to look across the pond to see more positive black representation across the arts in particular - music, TV, Film etc. Which meant that from my experience, British Black people of my generation were very Americanised due to a severe lack of representation and opportunity on our British shores that embodied our culture and more transparently, our appearance!

Thankfully for me, Uncle Phil and Sir Trevor weren't the only ones. Age 22 I got on the property ladder and purchased my first home, I needed some artwork for the blank walls, and decided to create a collage of my most inspirational black men that I admired, and I got it professionally made into a canvas that took centre stage in my home. At the time I thought I was just paying homage to people who I liked and respected, but it was more than that, I was filling a missing void and was harvesting more power from them than simply the joy of listening to the Thriller album or watching the other MJ majestically Hangtime in the air gracefully, more ballerina than Bull.

Martin Luther King, Malcolm X, Kanye West, Denzel Washington, Bob Marley, Michael Jackson, Muhammed Ali, Floyd Mayweather, Will Smith, Michael Jordan, Nelson Mandela - On the face of it these men are very contrasting and somewhat polarizing. However, they are more kindred spirits than what their respective impacts on the world would typically convey. They all had something to say, all of them masters of their craft and exceptional in their own rights, some civil, using their platform to say something meaningful, and doing so with conviction and without fear. I was drawn to that quality of strength, unwavering self-confidence, and character to voice their truth regardless of whether the opinion was popular or controversial, whilst in many instances knowing there would be life threatening consequences or negative backlash. These men who looked like me, in their own way helped give me confidence and whilst the tone, pitch, messaging or way they communicated may have sometimes missed the mark or appeared abrasive or muddled to the general public. I never missed the core and meaning of what they were trying to express and that it came from a pure hearted place with intent to make a positive difference. They all had a little something that I saw value in and that inspired me, 15 years later and different homes since then, I still have that canvass protected in bubble wrap, I can't bear to part with it, I never will, means too much and symbolizes even more.

I looked up at them every day, and to them, through my twenties and each in their own little way were fathers to me, teaching me life lessons and empowering me. They started movements, broke down barriers, evoked change, shaped culture, inspired, created art that is timeless, and some died for their cause and what they believed in. So, the rest of us that followed could prosper on a less oppressive road.

They taught me that, "our lives begin to end the day we become silent about things that matter", and that" a wise man can play the part of a clown but a clown can't play the part of a wise man", whilst "some people are so poor, all they have is money", and while "showing is better than telling", that "without commitment you'll never start, without consistency you'll never finish", but "if my mind can conceive it and my heart can believe it, then I can achieve it, impossible is nothing", however "if you quit once it becomes a habit, never quit", and that "greatness exists in us all" but that "there is no passion to be found playing small- in settling for a life that is less than the one you are capable of living" and "don't be afraid to be different" because "everything I'm not, made me everything I am". I thank them all for unsuspectingly stepping in as positive role models and sharing the role of dad to me!

Irrespective of those inspirational father figures sharing daddy duties, I was still lacking a consistent figurehead in my life with an Adams apple. There was no active male around to take me football on a Saturday morning, run the school dad race, teach me how to ride a bike, show me how to treat women, tell me about the birds and the bees or educate me on how to be a respectable man.

There was only broken promises, countless hours and days waiting at the bedroom window for him to show up and see me, but never arrive. The alluring bittersweet froth of an ice-cold pint of Guinness, would continually prove to be more appealing to him! My mum is superwoman and played the role of mum and dad to my sister and I, but as wonderful a job she did, it wasn't the same. My mother has told me my behaviour changed when my father left the household, I became aggressive, bad tempered and would often lash out. Learnt behaviour it seems. I acted out what I saw, 90% of the memories I have of my father, if I can call him that, are unfavourable ones. Child therapy helped me talk about it and deal with his absence and thankfully with the love of my mum and sister I came through those young formative years and used these experiences as unrelenting drive and fuel to succeed in life. But I'm going to be a dad, and I had no male to mirror or manifest any positive feelings of what a dad is, to in turn pass onto my unborn child.

I then quickly rid myself of these doubts and determined not to let my dad affect the brilliant father I intend to be, I vowed I would never make my child feel like I did and I would give them everything I didn't have. Material not materialistic, Stability, presence, male encouragement, discipline, time and most importantly, love.

I'm going to be a dad, the best news of my life!

6

CHAPTER TWO

~

First Sight

When I saw the list of things needed before baby arrived, I almost gave birth. I could see my bank balance draining before my eyes, Lauren was writing each item down with such joy, finding things that were not even essential and very quickly wants and nice to haves, became needs and I simply just had to accept that being logical and practical had no place in mums happy place, shopping. Thankfully I had fiscal reserves in place through habitual saving to limit the financial stress, so could smile and give Lauren the freedom to have whatever she felt was needed for baby. alleviate any possible restraints on what was, the most seismic event to happen in either of our lives. I would always find a way!

Anyone who I knew that had connections to get discounts in major retailers was getting contacted by me, I was pulling in the favours because 5% off here or 20% off there on big ticket items, made a huge difference. Which then left surplus funds for Lauren's extravagant 'nice to haves' gadgets. I was of course being sensible and frugal when buying my unborn child, a high-spec Dyson dehumidifying machine, that could regulate and set desired temperature, purify air, oscillating whilst omitting selected cool or hot air, and tell us what toxins are in the atmosphere then consequently rid the room of unwanted particles automatically. I mean, that was me being wholly practical, sensible, and responsible, not getting carried away with the excitement of becoming a parent, only the essentials of course!

Within three months I had already got the buggy, pram, basket, car seat, baby monitor and everything else that was necessary and on the 'nice to haves' fun list. I was a man possessed, ensuring Lauren and I had everything needed to care for our baby. The only things we didn't get were clothes because we didn't know what colours we would need, the thought of such an exciting colourful experience being placated by the neutrality of beige was not an option, so we would wait to find out if we were having a girl or boy.

Lauren and I had talked about whether we wanted to find out the sex of our baby or keep it as a surprise. I certainly wanted to find out so I could get a head-start on visualising what he/she would look like. To give me some knowing in what was a journey into the unknown, finding out the baby gender would mean getting first sight of the little person inside of Lauren who I would be dad to. We both agreed we wanted to know and at week 20 we arrived at the hospital to meet our developing little baby. It was a peach at this stage, I was checking the highly competitive fruit and veg markets each week when trading opened, to see what size the baby would be at each timeline then buying that actual fruit or vegetable and placing it on my desk at work. Lauren was unaware I was doing this, but it was my unique way of being connected to the baby, growing with baby each week by holding and visualizing that apple or pear for 7 days until it would evolve into something else.

Once again, I was left, sat on a chair, shunned on the outside on the wrong side of the door, whilst Lauren was being quizzed on whether I was controlling, abusive and a danger to her and baby. I had been on chairs like this a multitude of times for various check-ups or meetings, certainly not the right kind of vibe or positive energy a dad-to-be wants to walk into, especially on a day where the gender of baby is to be revealed.

Completely understand the process is for safeguarding reasons, and that this layer of confidentiality and safe space for women is an important necessity, but it still didn't negate the imposters syndrome feeling that stirred within me, and that this constant separation of dad from mum and bump at key stages throughout the pregnancy journey creates not only an isolation feeling but a real physical action of dads being shut out of rooms and made to wait on the side-lines. It's not a nice experience and the ward may as well have had a sign saying, "dad free zone", I thought, huge over exaggeration, but the frustration that was building up inside me was becoming deeply profound, it shouldn't be this hard to want to be completely involved.

After about five minutes or so, the door opened and the nurse invited me in, Lauren was already laying down on the bed and I sat beside her. The nurse talked through what he would be examining and that he would point things out on a tv screen that was positioned close to us and explain what he was checking. He proceeded to give Lauren some ultrasound gel to rub over her belly, it was so surreal, I had seen this happen countless times before on tv, the nurse then turned the screen on and placed the scanner on Lauren's belly.

Moments later black and white pixels and static sounds appeared on the screen followed by a noise that was ten times faster than a normal heartbeat, the nurse explained that was perfectly typical. The image then began to formulate and become clear, our baby then appeared to take centre stage, first sight! I looked at Lauren and she was already in tears, I was stunned, completely overwhelmed. This was our baby moving and floating around inside Laurens belly, looking like an alien but he/she was our special creation and being. The doctor proceeded to take detailed measurements of every organ and body part, before confirming whether we would like to know the sex of the baby.

He asked what we thought the gender might be, "girl" Lauren said passionately, I nodded in agreement, the nurse then said, "he is all legs". "He", I said, "so it's a boy?", "yes" he replied, pointing to our son's private parts on the screen, following up with "he's definitely a boy". So, I was going to be a dad, to a son, I needed a moment to take it all in and began choking up, when that lump in the throat begins to get bigger and starts to hurt when you are suppressing the need to let out your emotions. The nurse then printed baby scan images of our boy, which I couldn't stop staring at, scrutinising every single feature, "he's definitely got my forehead" I said about thirty times, followed by, "the nurse said he is all legs, so he's going to be tall just like his daddy".

By the time we left and got to the car park, I had mapped out his entire life straight to the NBA where he would be a basketball phenomenon. Lauren snapped me back to reality, but the paternal instinct to protect, provide and be selfless was immediate and felt the most natural thing for me to feel in the world. Purpose, I couldn't get the comment the nurse said out of my head as I drove us home, "he is all legs", I was tall just like my father was, so that description resonated with me acutely and unexpectedly, a direct comparison formed through DNA, but the match wouldn't just end there like it did for me. A list started to form on those empty pages of my childhood, experiences that I didn't have with my father that my son automatically would with me, many experiential but most also emotive based, centered around validation and stability, a knowing. My son knowing that he has a dad that will be in his corner, a knowing of safety and security that will breed a deeper level of confidence, and a knowing that his dreams, aspirations, and goals will be supported by someone who looks like him and loves him. A role model, an example, a dad.

I now had a baby scan image of my boy that could sit on my desk at work, alongside whatever harvest my son transformed into each week which would be a fruitful sight I looked forward to seeing.

CHAPTER THREE

~

Hypnobirthing

Lauren had the perfect start to pregnancy, no morning sickness or fatigue. As a soon to be dad I wanted to ensure I attended every neonatal meeting, check-ups, and scans. Being passive was not an option, I wanted to give Lauren all the support in the world and be active and involved.

I found many of the classes attended very frustrating, dad's role in the pregnancy process is often reduced to holding the birthing bag and counting contractions with a stopwatch, as opposed to any deep meaningful contribution to the birthing process that makes us feel empowered and equally as important. Nor do the classes delve into a dad's fears and insecurities that could be things other than the birth, such as money, support, fear or getting the wheels in motion to provide a safe home for new to be family. In my case I was selling and buying a property and was under time pressures to get things in place before the due date, I also got a promotion at work so had to deal with the self-expectation to succeed in that new role and handle business whilst providing a stress-free platform for Lauren and baby to thrive. To say all these factors challenged my mental health would be an understatement and I would later find

12

bottling these emotions inside and carrying this immense load would have consequences.

Then came Hypnobirthing, this was something Lauren had asked we do, there were many different options however we chose one highly recommended on a few of the local mum forums locally and on Instagram, London hypnobirthing, the course was run by director Hollie de Cruz. Now I can confess, I was very sceptical about hypnobirthing and would often make sarcastic comments and silly jokes. I had visions of it being meditation fused with scientology cult-like propaganda and hypnosis, with a generous sprinkle of witchcraft. However, I was pleasantly surprised, there was a profound emphasis on the birthing partners being as actively involved in all aspects of the birthing process. A clear and structured educational course with positive word association, phrasing, visualisation, and relaxation techniques to help strip away elements of fear surrounding childbirth. Fear built up by the over dramatization of the birthing experience on TV that show the process being frantic, scary and wholly traumatic, more akin to horror than the beauty and essence of life, for our viewing pleasure of course.

Surges would become a phrase that really resonated with me, the term is used to replace the word contractions to better describe the deep intense and powerful feeling that women experience during childbirth. This word would symbolically represent the wave of emotions I would experience throughout this journey as a would-be dad.

Hypnobirthing provided plenty of tips for dads to help feel prepared and a little empowered, to create a safe space and environment for mum and baby, it gave the other dads and I on the course a sense of importance and what felt like a central role to play. Being in a leadership sales role in my work life, I am used to driving things forward, controlling situations and adding immense value, but in the baby process I felt vulnerable and helpless. So, being able to be given a pivotal lead role in the biggest situation in my life was immense for me and appreciated, I mean, how many dads throw the towel in and walk away because they think they are not needed? Or relationships breaking down due to some men feeling they are not important as baby is getting all the attention that used to be on them?

There was some over the top, loud orgasmic noises, and 'banter' from a few of the would-be dads who thought they were comedians on the breathing exercises, but that made for a few light-hearted laughs and sighs from the mums. Hypnobirthing provides a valuable toolbox, I wouldn't use all the tools in there but as and when needed, there would always be something that could be of benefit, or so I thought. This added to my growing feelings of being involved, prepared, confident and excited. Then came Amsterdam.... Damn!!

CHAPTER FOUR

~

Amster-Damn

It's referred to as the babymoon, a celebratory vacation, similar to a honeymoon but without the vows, white dress, or embarrassing best man speech. One last trip away as a couple before the birth of first child or can use the word parent to describe yourself. Call it the last dance, the encore, last hoorah... the final curtain call before an exciting new life begins.

Amsterdam is the Netherlands' capital, known for its artistic heritage, intricate canal system and narrow houses with gabled facades, legacies of the city's 17th-century Golden Age. That's the cultured summary, in truth cannabis cafes with a Willy Wonka array of edible delights, Anne Frank's extraordinary diary and a red-light district where women smile & wave at you from windows were what first sprung to mind. Truly welcoming city indeed, but not exactly the most wholesome of settings to symbolise our babymoon. Nonetheless, beautiful walks along the river, fabulous restaurants and the enchanting Christmas markets were enough to convince us to go.

Before setting off, Lauren had gone to the GP to check her blood pressure and make sure everything was ok because she had experienced a little swelling. Being a specially qualified trained doctor from her minutes of experience on Google search, Lauren had self-diagnosed herself with Preeclampsia. GP ruled this out and gave us the ok to travel, with our minds at ease we set off to Amsterdam.

We decided on Eurostar as our mode of transport, a nice comfortable straightforward journey, we had thought about plane but the intensified risk of increased blood pressure and blood clots due to high altitude quickly ruled that out. I did strangely suffer from frequent aggressive turbulence on the Eurostar journey, but Lauren later confessed it was her shoving me in the ribs due to my excessively loud and embarrassing snoring.

We successfully checked into our hotel, put bags down and began our tour of the city, we had already planned various sightseeing activities and in the first two days we visited all the iconic landmarks, Anne Frank Museum was harrowing, the canal walks were lovely, we took photos by the spectacular 100-foot Christmas tree in the main square and the winter markets were just what we expected. I was boozy on mould wine and content with all the lovely street food to offer but throughout the trip there was an underlying niggling concern as Lauren was feeling constantly tired, slight headache, fatigued and experiencing puffiness around her ankles. Being the sympathetic partner I am, I started rapping some of puff daddy's biggest hits with real attitude whilst naming her puff mummy, she saw the funny side and referenced the song "I'll be missing you" indicating if I continued, I wouldn't be alive much longer. My humour was just masking my worries that were bubbling inside. So, on the penultimate day of the trip, we chilled out enjoying and relaxing in our hotel then went out to an amazing two Michelin Star restaurant in the evening that engaged all our senses and taste buds, then decided to take a slow walk back to our hotel.

Halfway through the journey and near Amsterdam Centraal station we stumbled across a vibrant part of the city called 'De Wallen', with an eclectic mix of people and enterprising atmosphere, we later found out we were in the blue light district which is a transgender hub for sex workers. Few canals turn later we were in the heart of one of the most infamous tourist attractions in Europe, The Red-light district. In truth I found it seedy and unnerving, my inner sense of danger and alertness was at maximum level, I certainly did not see the pleasure there. I started to think about my unborn child and what if they succumb to this illicit underworld whilst painfully aware that many of the women in these windows waving for custom were not there by choice. I could see the sadness in their eyes behind the counterfeit alluring smiles, they are commodities controlled by crime rings for drugs, slavery and ultimately profit. Many of the cash – sex transactions we saw along our swift walk were overseen by menacing men in large groups supervising their business and human livestock nearby.

These places exist in every city around the world and at least Amsterdam have tried to regulate it for safety, but there was something very disturbing about the direct hard-hitting openness and desensitization that almost legitimises and numbs the vulgarity of what you are witnessing which does leave you questioning your core values and morality. We saw a raucous stag-do enter one of the premises and noticed there were purple lights flashing in the windows. Google then informed us that the purple light indicated the sex workers were transvestite. I don't know if that stag were aware because drunken shouts of "come on lads let's do her" suggest not, but being in the Netherlands, I am confident all would have been revealed once sexual explorations arrived down to the Nether regions.

Overwhelmed by bold red, purple and blue, Lauren and I both needed the serenity and harmony of tranquillity green…. little did I know that the red-light would be a warning for what was to come.

We arrived back at the hotel, vision blurred from our colourful journey home, we started getting ready for an early night but then Lauren started feeling pain in her right rib which progressively got worse and worse. She was pacing up and down the hotel room in pain, and we were now in full panic mode. "Is the baby ok?" Lauren said, she couldn't remember when she had last felt kicking or movement from baby, I could see the fear and worry in her face and inside I was petrified.

That red light warning was on full flashing panic alert, we started moving around and poking bump to get baby moving. After ten minutes of mummy gymnastics Lauren felt kicking which was a massive sigh of relief, though clearly something was wrong. We called St George's hospital back in London and Lauren told them that she thinks she may have pre-eclampsia having matched all the symptoms associated with the condition, the uncertainty was that these same symptoms are what you would expect in normal pregnancy which caused doubt for us. The nurse said "absolutely not" to our proposed diagnosis "as it would have been picked up already" instead suggesting it was probably baby in awkward position.

During the night I awoke in a dazed panic to the sound of flowing water, after initially believing I was drowning, I found Lauren was running a bath to try and relax due to the severe pain she was experiencing. She had also been vomiting, the right rib pain had resurfaced, and she had been up for last two hours trying to relieve the discomfort. Trying to find positions that help eased the pain such as the child's pose and downward facing dog pose, positions she had read about in baby books and learnt in neonatal classes. None of these postures were helping subside the painful throbbing but the bath had helped soothe and relax her a little, but I had already made the decision that we would be leaving Amsterdam early and I was up looking at earlier Eurostar trains back to London first thing in the morning so we could get to the hospital. The pit of my stomach was doing summersaults, watching the woman I love carrying our first baby in so much agony was extremely upsetting, I felt truly helpless offering only a brave face and comforting words of reassurance that everything would be fine. Not being able to control a situation and outcome left me vulnerable and exposed, the fear of wanting something so much and there being risk of it being taken away was too much to contemplate, so I suppressed and compartmentalised those thoughts and emotions. Defence mechanism I had been successful in engaging my whole life, self-preservation at its finest or just cowardly running away some would say. We raced back to London, Lauren went to her mums whilst I stopped off at home to drop off the bags, she then went straight to hospital with her mum which was located just round the corner, St Georges Hospital. Lauren then called me within the hour saying the doctors confirmed she was seriously ill and she would be staying in overnight so they could monitor her vital organs and a scan would need to be done to check baby was ok. Oh, the doctors diagnosed and confirmed that the pain she had been suffering, the fatigue, swelling around ankles and hands was indeed what Lauren had suspected despite twice being professionally told otherwise, pre-eclampsia!

CHAPTER FIVE

~

HELLP-lessness

The only time I had vaguely heard about pre-eclampsia was Lauren once mentioning that Kim Kardashian West had the condition when roping me into watching the reality show keeping up with the Kardashians. So my journey racing to the hospital, with my birthing bag I already had prepared safely in the boot, was spent listening to podcasts and YouTube videos discussing the condition, eventually having to turn it off as the potential consequences of this illness did not bare thinking about, silence was my passenger for the remainder of drive.

Reunited with Lauren, the doctors came into our cubicle to explain the results of the tests carried out and next steps. These tests involved taking Laurens blood pressure to ensure it wasn't too high, urine protein level test to make sure her kidneys were healthy, weight reading to gauge excess fluid retention, blood tests that included a complete blood count (CBC) in addition to checking creatinine levels and uric acid levels.

"You are very poorly" was how Dr Polly commenced the analysis, and that we should "get comfortable because we would be going nowhere anytime soon" she said with conviction, her tone serious and her expression grave. Lauren grabbed my hand and held it tight as we listened nervously to the test findings.

Laurens organs were in distress mode, her platelet count was severely below the normal number it should be, blood pressure had skyrocketed to 180 which was way above the 140 which is deemed dangerously high, kidneys and liver were failing, she had high levels of protein above 300mg in her urine and her blood count was low. In short, her body was completely shutting down!

The Dr then proceeded to explain what preterm preeclampsia was, though she may as well have been speaking Arabic or any other language foreign to me, because in that moment I couldn't understand a word of anything she was saying to us. My head was gone and my entire being was filled with utter dread, all I could think of was that two of the most important people in my life could be taken away from me in the cruellest and traumatic way, but I had to pull myself together and show strength and calmness.

We were given some reading material about what the condition was so that we could get our heads around it and understand the specifics and what the next stages of dealing with preeclampsia would look like.

Pre-eclampsia is a condition that affects some women, usually during the second half of pregnancy (from around 20 weeks) or soon after the baby is delivered. It is thought to be caused by the placenta not developing properly due to a problem with blood vessels supplying it, however the exact cause is not fully understood. Early signs of pre-eclampsia include having high blood pressure (hypertension) and protein in the urine (proteinuria), further symptoms can develop, including:

- Swelling of the feet, ankles, face, and hands caused by fluid retention (oedema)
- Severe headaches
- Vision problems
- Pain just below the ribs

These signs should be picked up during routine antenatal appointments, though should mothers notice any symptoms of pre-eclampsia, medical advice should be sought immediately. Although many cases are mild, the condition can lead to serious complications for both mother and baby if it's not monitored and treated. The earlier pre-eclampsia is diagnosed and monitored the better the outlook, Laurens view remained very unclear.

My immediate response to the doctors was frustration and anger, as Lauren had experienced pretty much all those associated symptoms and despite previously asking her GP whether she had pre-eclampsia before the trip to Amsterdam and then whilst abroad calling the hospital due to the pain she was in. On both occasions of seeking professional expert advice, pre-eclampsia was ruled out. Lauren was not listened to, and now we have to face upsetting uncertainty, when this could have detected early that undoubtedly would have prevented the illness getting worse.

The doctors said they would be performing these observation tests every four hours to monitor liver, heart rate and blood pressure. They were looking for stable consistent readings that would give them confidence to delay any need to induce early labour. The doctors then came back to our cubicle later that evening, following the results from further observation tests. Dr Polly said that Laurens results "showed no consistency and were all over the place", they couldn't "trust the data" and that we should prepare ourselves "for delivery of the baby in the coming days". Short, sharp and to the point, she also said before leaving that she believed that Lauren may have "the severe form of pre-eclampsia called HELLP Syndrome".

HELLP syndrome is a life-threatening pregnancy complication usually considered to be a variant of preeclampsia, both conditions usually occurring during the later stages of pregnancy.

HELLP syndrome was named by Dr. Louis Weinstein in 1982 after its characteristics:

1. H (haemolysis, which is the breaking down of red blood cells)
2. EL (elevated liver enzymes)
3. LP (low platelet count)

It can be difficult to diagnose, especially when high blood pressure and protein in the urine are not present. Its symptoms are sometimes mistaken for gastritis, flu, acute hepatitis, gall bladder disease, or other conditions. The morality rate of HELLP syndrome has been reported to be as high as 30%. That's why it's critical for expecting mothers to be aware of the condition and its symptoms so they can receive early diagnosis and treatment.

The physical symptoms of HELLP Syndrome may seem at first like preeclampsia. Pregnant women developing HELLP syndrome have reported experiencing one or more of these symptoms:

- Headache
- Nausea/vomiting/indigestion with pain after eating
- Abdominal or chest tenderness and upper right upper side pain (from liver distention)
- Shoulder pain or pain when breathing deeply
- Bleeding
- Changes in vision
- Swelling

I was shell-shocked and in a complete state of helplessness. What the hell was happening? less than 24 hours ago we were walking around the Christmas Markets in Amsterdam drinking a hot spiced apple beverage and eating cinnamon pretzels, and now we were in hospital with Lauren severely ill and being told that our baby may have to be delivered almost two months early.

It didn't make any sense to me, why out of nowhere things could suddenly go left when everything was going so right. Vocally and physically, I appeared reassuring, calm and confident about the situation. I was performing of course to pacify Laurens understandable anxiety, but on the inside, I was panicking, scared beyond belief and had no clue what the coming hour, day or weeks would look like. I felt so gutted and frustrated, I've always felt like I have had to fight for things, nothing I have achieved in my life has ever come easy and always I have had to overcome some sort of adversity to get just rewards. I don't know why I was stupid enough to think that an event as monumental as the birth of my first child would be smooth and without conflict. I was annoyed at myself that I had ignored my pattern of behaviour and completely let my guard down by fully investing emotionally into something where the desired outcome wasn't yet established.

Past experience has shown me that doing this only

increases the impact of disappointment should expectations, hope, or wants, not be met. Despite how I was feeling, I had to keep it internalized because Lauren must have been feeling 100 times worse and be totally petrified. This was happening to her, and she had been carrying our precious cargo inside her for over 7 months so the level of emotion and bond already formed would be indescribable. My emotions, feelings and fears rightfully took a backseat, I needed to be the pillar of positivity and an unmovable rock for her and our unborn child, manifesting and visualizing only optimistic thoughts and outcomes, I needed to be wholly selfless not selfish, and be whatever was required of me to be at any given stage of what was going to be a roller-coaster journey.

CHAPTER SIX

~

Blue Chair

Lauren and I were settling into our new environment and coming to terms with the dramatic past 24 hours, even if she had doubted it, I made it clear to her that I would be by her side at every step of the way, and she could rely on me 110%. One of the nurses had earlier mentioned that visiting hours ended at 10pm, I thought nothing of it as of course that didn't apply to me, and sure enough I saw a few visitors packing up saying their goodbyes as that time neared. Shortly after 10pm one of the nurses then came into our cubicle and said, "sorry sir, you'll have to leave now, visiting hours are over". In similar fashion to a scene from film Wolf of Wall Street, Jordan Belfort played by Leonardo DiCaprio, famously says "I'm not leaving".

In the same sprit but without the expletives I very calmly said "I'm sorry but I am not leaving Madam, I know you are just doing your job, but my partner is pregnant with my child and seriously unwell. So, you need to understand that there is no way in hell that I am leaving her side." I continued "I promise you; I won't make noise or cause any problems whatsoever. I will just sit here quietly in this blue chair beside my partner". Silence. She nodded, smiled and dragged back the curtain to our cubicle closed. I breathed a sigh of relief because any further resistance or insistence I vacate the building would have led me to go full DiCaprio mode screaming, with expletives, "I'm not fucking leaving, this is my home! They're gonna need a fucking wrecking ball to take me out of here!"

Blue chair was now my home, well, for the foreseeable future at least, and I embraced that realisation with conviction. You see, when you come from hardship, you become battle ready and accept the need to dig deep. This was the time to be in the trenches and I was ready to go to war with pre-eclampsia, HELLP syndrome, nurses, doctors and whoever else was getting in the way of allowing me to be a man, partner or father, being present to protect my family. Siege mentality had set in!

Over the next day or so, Lauren was having her observations, 'Obs' being the acronym, done every four hours, this was to monitor and collate a series of data that hopefully showed a pattern of stability rather than the fluctuating unpredictability which was concerning the doctors. Every day that passed without having to deliver the baby was another daily win that got us closer to the due date thus significantly improving the chances of survival should early delivery be needed.

Throughout the day I would be up early wandering around the hospital getting coffee and pastries from the canteen on the ground floor, my back ached from sitting in that chair all night and I struggled to get any real sleep so needed that walk to stretch out. Lauren and I would also go for a stroll to get her out of the bed and have our daily Pret a Manger lunch date, it was important we shared some normality to partially distract us from baby worries, but also an excuse for me to have the steak mac & cheese which was ridiculously good.

We would often sit in Pret and people watch, see the doctors and nurses running in and out grabbing a sandwich on the go to rush back to perform miracle work. The various different patients, visitors, workers all going through their own personal battles and worries which often gave us solace in the fact that there is always someone else going through something similar or worse than you. We weren't alone, Christmas decorations were up all over the hospital, festive songs playing and thousands of people who would want to be celebrating the holidays at home with family but were in St Georges Hospital just like us.

Also found out the blue chair reclined, felt like I had won the lottery, my legs still dangled off the end but to be able to lay down gave me a win, a very small win which is so significant when you feel as if you are just taking a multitude of losses.

I always save and take majority of my work annual leave holiday in December, you see, Christmas is my favourite time of year and this one would certainly be the most memorable. I love everything about this festive holiday, I've always been more excited to give presents than receive buts it's the nostalgic traditions and family time that I really love about this time of year and hold sacred.

Growing up as a child, there were no games consoles, popular branded trainers, and designer label clothes, instead there was a big turkey with all the trimmings, cornbread, ackee and salt fish, rice and peas, Carrot juice and bammy. All made with love and more notably it's how Christmas made us feel. But when you're young, you're just thinking about the latest popular toy or thing that all your other friends will have but you wouldn't and it's tough to accept or understand at the time. Though I always knew my mum was doing the best she could for my sister and I, I saw the unbelievable work ethic, discipline, and commitment of putting us first. Before anyone else, including herself, sacrifice!

Every year I get my mum a real Norwegian tree, no shedding of needles in our household, Christmas carols play aloud and with me singing "let it snow" by Boys II Men, it's always just my mum, sister and I, when I was younger I used to wish I had a bigger family, but I value the three of us spending quality time together with mum and sister bickering and me getting away with doing absolutely nothing except stuffing my face with pigs in blankets. My mum makes sorrel every year and finally gave me the secret recipe a few years back, so we go head-to-head to see whose is the best, Sorrel is a Jamaican drink. Similar to mould wine but with rum, cloves, and plenty of ginger to pack a punch, can also make it without alcohol, it's the perfect evening drink with some cheese, olives and crackers with the Christmas tree lights on and a film, nothing beats Miracle on 34th street. It encapsulates the spirit of Christmas, understanding the magic and excitement, kids especially feel about Christmas, more apt this year as I was unexpectedly going to be a father in the coming days and most likely be spending Christmas day in St Georges Hospital, on my blue chair. This Christmas would be different!

CHAPTER SEVEN

~

Christmas Day

"Merry Christmas cub" followed by a kiss from me on Laurens bump was how my Christmas morning began. Throughout Laurens pregnancy we nicknamed the baby cub, which is what the young of felines in the animal kingdom are called. I would play a game called boom boom. Which basically involved me lightly tapping the belly with my fist, like a boxer would on the pads, whilst saying "boom boom boom" and then cub would copy and tap back three times or however many times I boom boomed. I must have tapped the belly 30 times waiting for cub to wake up and answer my calls, I needed that reassurance that all was well and there was movement. He responded, I then got us a special Christmas morning malted drink from the hot drink station in the ward hallway, I knew today was going to be memorable, so I gave us a few extra scoops of Malt to get us on our merry way.

I left Lauren's by her bedside as she was still half asleep and set off at the crack of dawn back home to have a shower, and to collect Laurens Christmas presents so that she could open them at the hospital. I had to try and provide some sort of normality and to make Christmas Day as special as possible considering the circumstances, extra few scoops of malted powder simply wouldn't cut it!

Few hours later I made it back to our cubicle and Lauren was upright sipping on her now cold - Malt milkshake. I had still made it back before 10am, but slightly delayed as I had stopped off at my mums to collect presents her and my sister had got Lauren to add to the sack of goodies she could open.

Lauren was on FaceTime to her family, whom I assumed were just wishing her Merry Christmas but would see her shortly. Instead, I saw that they were opening up their Christmas presents while Lauren watched on her phone. I was incensed, her family only lived 10 minutes down the road. Why couldn't they have just come to the hospital and opened presents with Lauren and made it special for her. I had just done a two hour round trip to try and give her some morning happiness. Am I the only one who is thinking about her and understands the severity of what is going on? I thought. I simply didn't get it and was furious with them but didn't want to vocalise my disappointment too much, so not to upset Lauren. Her family said they were coming early afternoon to bring us Christmas Dinner, so told my mum not to, instead she would come later in the afternoon with her delicious sorrel I was so looking forward to.

All the restaurants and cafes were closed for Christmas, so we were desperately salivating for food like wild hyenas. I was running low on breakfast protein bar snacks courtesy of my birthing bag, so had to start rationing portions so we could survive till the cavalry came to provide lunch. We were in the trenches of our own little war!

When lunch finally came at 4pm, sigh, we devoured it, my mum then came shortly afterwards with the sorrel, and we all sat in the seating area of the ward. There is never a quiet moment when Laurens family is around which was welcomed and much needed, their zest for life, enthusiasm and fun fused with my family's nurturing, thoughtful and unconditional love. When combined made for a powerful dynamic and perfect balance.

Whilst we were all chatting, I noticed a man entering one of the private rooms with a clear vision and purpose, shortly afterwards he began getting to work.

I recognised the control and prepared organisation he was projecting in the way he was going about his business, Hypnobirthing. He had a bag of hypnobirthing tools fully at his disposal, and he came into the room to set up and create the perfect environment that he and his partner had visualised. He proceeded to light the scented candles, turning on his mini speaker with calming spa sounds, he lined up refreshments, sweets, and fruits on the side, along with stress relieving objects he placed around the room, he was even checking the temperature of the water in the bath, which was more like an inflatable hot tub, to ensure it was at the perfect climate predetermined. He then took a step back and surveyed his masterpiece, once he was happy with how he positioned everything after a few minor but precise adjustments, he checked his watch then dimmed the lights down. Everything was running like clockwork, and then came the main event, his pregnant partner walking down the hallway with the midwife and stepping into the perfect environment she and he had created. It was beautiful.

Lauren and I looked on in awe and a little jealously because we were witnessing the birth experience we had envisioned and wanted, why couldn't we have had such a beautifully orchestrated symphony of a birth? Instead of the chaotic chorus of unpredictability we were going through, just wishing we were tone deaf to it all.

"Not because it's for everyone else it must mean it is for you" another Caribbean saying I grew up hearing, used many a time by my mum. In truth, we were happy to see another couple having their special moment, it was like they were having it for us as well.

After a few hours, Lauren seemed lethargic, so our family went home to provide her with some rest. We went back to our cubicle to chill out and watch Eastenders on our iPad, that show always provided Christmas Day fireworks and mayhem, but nothing could top the drama that was about to happen to us.

CHAPTER EIGHT

~

The Starry Night

Christmas evening there was a shift in atmosphere and Laurens health, she had started to re-experience some of the HELLP symptoms, so the nurses were doing more checks and tests on her, feeling somewhat scared and helpless I told Lauren I was just nipping out to the hallway to get a hot malted drink that I had become so fond of, it's funny the little things you find comfort in.

From the window of our hospital ward, I gazed out to the star filled night sky with bright full moon to capture a brief moment of calm and stillness from the turmoil and emotional whirlwind that was taking place, I then immediately thought of 'The Starry Night'. Whilst in Amsterdam, Lauren and I had had visited the Van Gogh Museum and spent a long time looking at his iconic works while the tour guide broke down the meaning and history behind each painting with passion, emotion and in an engaging story telling way. This particular masterpiece really resonated with me during these moments gazing out at the sky, symbolic of my feelings and strained state of mind evoking strong emotions from the vivid feel of the painting.

Vincent Van Gogh painted "Starry Night" in 1889 from a hospital room in the mental asylum at Saint-Remy where he was recovering from mental illness and his ear amputation. In the painting, the tree reaches into the sky, experts depict it serving as a direct connection between the earth and the heavens. The heavens were where I was looking up to praying to God that everything would turn out positively for us, I would happily in that moment have cut my own ear off like Van Gogh did or any other part of my body if it meant erasing the pain Lauren was going through and ensuring her and baby were alright.

The turbulent play of light and dark in "Starry Night" have been compared to the mathematical expression of turbulence in such natural occurrences as whirlpools and air streams. It is suggested that since the artist created these particular artworks during periods of extreme mental agitation, Van Gogh was uniquely able to accurately communicate that agitation using precise shades of luminescence. This explains why, when I thought about that painting it stirred such sentiment in me, as the turbulent nature of what Lauren and I were going through felt like a roller-coaster or twister being shaken around with our nerves on a knife-edge.

Research has confirmed that the dominant morning star in the painting is actually the planet Venus, which was in a similar position at the time Van Gogh was working on "Starry Night," and it would have shone brightly, just as Van Gogh painted it. They say women are from Venus, in

Greek mythology Venus was the goddess of love and fertility, the parallels between that painting and my current mood were impossible to ignore and gave me Goosebumps. Not a star, but the love in my heart for Lauren carrying our child was precisely what I was thinking about when I was looking up at that bright full moon, who would have thought our babymoon would represent such a theatrical turn of events neither of us could have foreseen? I just remained hopeful that the outcome at the final curtain call would be a standing ovation to the sounds of a crying healthy new-born and tears of joy, a bad ending may well have Van Gogh and I being even more intertwined. My office at work is located a few streets away from where Van Gogh lived for a year in London. On the 27th July 1890, he shot himself in the chest dying of the injuries a few days later, he was 37 years old, my birthday shares the same day and month of his suicide, and I would be 37 years old the following year. Scary or should I say Starry.

Snapping out my Van Gogh starry gaze, Laurens health was seriously taking a turn for the worse, the painkillers the nurses were giving her were not helping and Lauren was becoming more and more uncomfortable. I had seen these postures for comfort she was trying before in Amsterdam, and she asked me to run the shower on in the communal bathroom on ward to see if that would help the pain. It was at this time I knew that our child would most likely have to be delivered in the coming days if not hours. HELLP syndrome had stopped playing games and was letting us know it wasn't going anywhere soon. Sure enough the latest round of 'Obs' showed Laurens vital organs deteriorating, and Lauren's pain intensifying. Her body was crying for Help.

CHAPTER NINE

~

Cry For HELLP

"Babe, I'm in so much pain, this is worse than in Amsterdam" the tears were flowing from Lauren, HELLP had fully taken over her body. She had a lot of the symptoms associated with the syndrome to a heightened level; blurry vision, pain in upper right part of belly, headaches, fatigue, nausea and the swelling had returned, but thankfully no seizures or bleeding but she was in a very poorly state.

Lauren was crying for HELLP to subside and go away; I was again in a state of helplessness. "It will be ok babe, you're doing well" I would repeatedly tell Lauren. The nurses increased Lauren's dosage of painkillers to try and ease the pain, the doctor on duty then came into see us. He said should the symptoms continue; we would need to have another scan of baby then potentially move downstairs in preparation of early delivery.

Two hours later, we were having a scan of baby, our nerves were rattled. Thankfully all was well but there would be risk delivering almost two months early. We headed back to our cubicle but through the night the pain was getting even more severe, and Lauren couldn't sleep or get comfortable. Strictly come dancing would never have seen the variety of moves Lauren was showing off, as she tried to find a position of comfort. One of the other doctors came and informed us we were moving a floor down to the maternity ward where mothers are prepared in readiness for childbirth.

They hooked Lauren up to machines and gave her a small dose of morphine to try and get her comfortable. We had to get through the night and early hours as the doctors don't like to do emergency C sections or operations when the human body is in a state of trauma. HELLP was ravaging Lauren and her vital organs needed to stabilise before delivery of baby could be attempted in a safer way. 2-4am could only described as witching hours of extreme worry, Lauren was now constantly vomiting as a result of the pain.

I was trying to use calming hypnobirthing techniques I had learnt to try and relax her. However, she didn't appreciate my attempts at making swirly round shapes with my finger along her back and said, "what the hell are you trying to do Paul, STOP IT you idiot". To be fair I could have had a more circular stroke to my technique.

Luckily the morphine started to kick in and she was finally able to settle a little. A few hours later Dr Ruth popped into the room and confirmed that Lauren would be delivering the baby today and they would try and encourage a natural birth via pessary, to try and induce labour.

The pessary, which is inserted into the vagina, looks like a very small tampon/tablet. It contains Prostaglandins which are released slowly over 24 hours to ripen the cervix. (NHS.UK)

I then went into the hallway to gather my thoughts; I was going to be a father today so beyond excited. But also, vividly aware that the timing and situation was far from ideal, so fear and nerves were an understatement of what I was feeling. I called my mum and told her that she would be meeting her grandson today and for her to come to the hospital ASAP. "Remember, god doesn't give you more than you can bear" she said before hanging up. A familiar passage from the bible that was repeated throughout our lives when we would go through the choppy waters that life brings.

Next call was my sister, same message. "You're about to meet your nephew, come to the hospital ASAP". One of the best things about the festive period is switching off mentally from the 9-5 routine of work. Losing track of what day it is, as our sense of time is distorted. I didn't know what planet I was currently on never mind what day it was, my sister would remind me.

"Oh, he clearly likes an occasion" she said, "what do you mean" I replied, "It's Boxing Day today bruv, this will always be an expensive year for you now" she said whilst laughing. She was right of course but I immediately smiled, as what better time of year for family to come together and celebrate. Creating even more special memories.

It felt symbolic that he would be coming into the world through adversity and fighting, whilst also tinged with literal irony, as throughout Lauren's pregnancy I would pretend box her belly playfully like Floyd Mayweather on the speed ball and now my son would be "boom boom booming" his way into the world. What a day to do it, December 26th, Boxing   Day.

CHAPTER TEN

~

Heart Stone

My sister is a strong, spiritual, and positive black woman, when I saw her, she immediately ran to me and gave me a big hug, I wanted to burst into tears and show my vulnerabilities and fear, but I couldn't. Laurens family were in the room, and I had to appear strong and in control of my emotions, I couldn't show weakness. This is the toxic masculinity babble I told myself anyway, but big sis could always see through me, growing up if I ever got into trouble, which is was most of the time, I would always go to her first before the issue got to my mum. Lisa would then back me so that the consequence was never in reality quite as bad as the feared anticipated outcome. To this day, she can look at me and tell something is wrong, her positive energy was so desperately needed, and she came bearing a special gift. Timely, as after all it is Boxing Day, a festive holiday originated to give gifts to the poor, very apt considering how poorly Lauren was, any token of kindness or festive cheer that could change our fortunes was greatly welcomed.

It wasn't gold, frankincense, and myrrh like the gifts the three wise men gave baby Jesus, far more precious. It was a heart shaped crystal made from rose quartz, it had been given to my sister by her best friend Tasha who had very sadly passed away some years before from sadness of the heart. Her heart had suddenly stopped due to a condition called SAD Syndrome, Sudden Adult Death Syndrome, so this rose quartz had a powerful and special importance to Lisa, but she felt like Lauren, and I needed it, she was right. It could have been a pebble found in the gravel of the hospital car park, it gave me hope and something tangible to literally cling onto other than my faith in God.

My sister wasn't the only one with gifts to offer...

My mum had travelled in a taxi, due to busses being run on a slow and restricted bank holiday service, carrying two big bags of gifts with her, to the hospital. But just like growing up, these weren't gifts feeding into the commercialism of Christmas, these gifts would fill the heart, nourish the mind and feed the soul, these were gifts that served a higher power. Despite knowing I wouldn't be spending Christmas Day with her this year due to the unforeseen change of plans; this didn't stop her from cooking up a culinary banquet, she must have known we would all need her soul food and amazing grace.

The room was silent, just the occasional moans of satisfaction that could have been mistaken for ravenous hyenas devouring their prey, which would break the silence every so often. There were smiles and regular nods of approval and for a very brief moment, I had a sense of escapism as I poured the savoury-sweet cranberry gravy over my Turkey and pigs in blankets. We may have been in a hospital, but my mum had successfully made that waiting room a home, which was unquestionably her intention. She would have been forgiven for dishing out the food on paper plates considering the circumstances and we all would have been equally appreciative and thought nothing of it, but this was my mother. She had brought along her finest sterling silver cutlery set and China porcelain plates with full accompanying set of side dishes and serving plates, simply incredible. These were familiar family items and actions that would truly resonate with me at this momentous time, she even brought festive napkins, true silver service indeed! Typical mum, "if you're going to do something then do it well and to the best of your ability", this was the mantra she instilled in my sister and me.

My mother would continually put others before herself, to her detriment at times, she is strong, kind, considerate and would do absolutely anything for her children. If, like the buses, there were no taxi services running, I could bet my life that she would have walked the 10-mile journey to the hospital. Because nothing would stop her from supporting me and being there to greet her first grandchild into the world, nothing!

Soon after Lisa and my mother's arrival, Dr Polly came into our room, which generally meant the level of seriousness went up a few significant notches, she was joined by two other fellow doctors. They came to explain the emergency caesarean procedure and potential risks, Laurens mum was also present in the room. I had started to dread seeing Dr Polly, treating her as if she was the grim reaper, bearing bad news and taking our souls, but eventually came to really appreciate the honesty, directness, and no fluff approach. She was preparing us for the worse and managing our expectations, giving us professional advice, informing us of the potential consequences and full transparency of the severity of the situation. I respected that more than she will ever know as it readied and focused my mentality to go to war. However, nothing quite prepares you for when they inform your partner that she could die during the procedure and that she will need to sign forms giving authority for them to conduct the C-section and permission if she wants to donate her organs should the worse happen.

At this point, Laurens mum is understandably beside herself with worry and the tears are flowing but I am consciously not engaging eye contact or entertaining the hysterics, it's not about her. I need to be the rock of reassurance and positivity for Lauren and don't want her to be anymore scared and worried than she already is, but my heart, soul and emotions were completely broken when Lauren asked the doctors "if I die, will I know I've died and feel it?, "no" the doctors replied, all I wanted to do was cry and hug her and bump tightly and not let go. Doctors shortly left after informing us that the operation would be taking place within the next thirty minutes, I followed the doctors out of the room and cornered one of them in the hallway, the one who would be delivering my baby. He must have felt like has being interrogated by FBI the way I was firing questions at him, how long have you been a doctor? How many caesarean procedures have you carried out? Have you had enough sleep; I need you on top form Dr? Do you need a drink? Mum and baby are going to be ok, right Dr? RIGHT DR? I feel sorry for him, loading that additional pressure on him wasn't fair but it was a petrified, emotional dad-to-be wanting comfort and reassurance. My entire world was in that room and one misplaced tired stroke of a scalpel could end it!

I bounced back into the room with synthetic positive energy, giving Lauren exaggerated versions of my conversation, if you can call it that, with the Dr, "yeh babe, spoke to the Dr and he said we have nothing to worry about, he does this loads of times a day, did a million of them yesterday, everything will be fine, he told us don't even sweat it". Anything to calm her nerves and breed confidence I was doing, it worked.

We decided to take some photos together, amidst all the worry and fear, we had to remind ourselves we were shortly going to meet our first baby, and this was a time for happiness and joy, at the back of my mind though these photos could also potentially be the last ones of us together should the unthinkable occur. One of the first things I purchased when I found out Lauren was pregnant was a Fujifilm polaroid camera, reminiscent of the type our grandparents used to have but modernised for hipster millennials. The old school polaroid ones where you closed one eye to focus and blinded people from the insanely bright flash, then spent ten minutes flapping the photo around until the picture magically appeared. Nostalgic indeed, the camera was recommended by some of the mums I dealt with at work, and I used to see them around homes when carrying out market appraisals, I had been taking polaroid's of Laurens bump every two weeks highlighting the week number and visually charting the size of bump growing which made for great fridge decoration. We were now at week 34, so took the final photo of Lauren holding baby bump and some happy ones with her and I, we then shared an intimate moment alone before the nurses came back in the room to say, "it's time" and take Lauren to theatre. I was not allowed in the theatre which I was annoyed about, but they arranged for me to be in a room directly opposite. They said I was allowed one person to join me, I declined, Laurens mum kindly said she would come if I wanted, I politely declined.

The magnitude of what was happening meant I only wanted my own thoughts, silence, and the safe space to feel, pray and emotionally vent however I wanted to, without having to deal with the feelings and presence of another human being. No distraction would help, I was locked in. Both sets of family were able to say good luck as she was wheeled through the corridor, I was allowed to stay with her till they got to the theatre doors, on arrival I kissed her and said "I love you" a hundred times before letting them take her away, I was then taken to the room opposite. The C-section would take roughly 35 minutes the Doctors said, I gave one of the nurses my mobile phone so they could take photos of baby upon delivery as we would miss those cherished first moments, someone would then come and get me to see mum and child.

Those thirty-five minutes felt like a lifetime, time surely stopped. I held tightly onto heart stone in the middle of palms of both hands praying to God that my family would survive and come out of his healthy. I also started repenting every sin I had ever committed in my life, from stealing penny sweets from local corner shop when I was ten years old to more grown-up shenanigans I got away with, I confessed all. I was all over the place, at my most vulnerable I ever have been in my life, a complete mess, I went from repeatedly pacing up and down the room talking to myself aloud affirming that everything would be fine. To then sitting in the corner on the floor crying, pleading, and praying to not only my god, but Allah, Greek mythical god Zeus, Buddha and any other spiritual higher power that could have positive influence over this outcome, I was exhausted and sweating "it must almost be time now, been in here for bloody ages". I checked my watch, only three minutes had passed, "no fucking way man". In the end, heart stone calmed my nerves, it also started emitting thermal energy, so I felt like it was connecting with me and communicating that we were in this together. Sounds crazy right? This was my mental state, I was treating this stone like the red Kryptonite that gave superman increased powers, but as mad as it may seem it ultimately helped get me through the next twenty minutes, the last twelve could only be described as mental hell.

Silence was abruptly broken by the sound of doors to the theatre room crashing open with nurses running out down the hallway with one shouting "we need assistance, get more nurses quick", que the most purest form of panic you'll ever see, I went bursting out the room I was in, chasing those same doctors down the hallway "excuse me, is my partner and baby ok?, tell me what the hell is going on in there", "calm down sir" one of the nurses replied, "we are not operating on your partner", "so what's happening in that room, she's in there supposed to be having a caesarean" I said. No one had thought to tell me that there would be numerous different procedures taking place on many patients within the same theatre room, so thankfully the commotion was not related to my family but was frightening nonetheless that another patient was clearly in serious trouble. Shortly after returning to my room, I heard the theatre doors open again, this time a female voice saying "has anyone spoken to dad?", one of the nurses the came in with a big smile on her face saying "everything went well, baby boy has arrived, we will be taking him to the intensive care unit now so follow us down", huge relief and excitement, but "how is Lauren" I asked, "they are still working on her, we will let you know as soon as we can". This was the strangest feeling, being on a monumental happy high that my baby boy has arrived and I'm about to meet him for the first time, to crashing back down to a state of intense anxiety because I didn't know if Lauren was ok and healthy. "My new-born son is the most important person right now and comes first" my first selfless thought as a parent, putting my child's needs and safety as number one priority, above everything and everyone, even Lauren.

I entered a room with six other babies in incubators, glass boxes with little humans inside, "sorry dad you can't touch him yet" they transferred my son into one of the incubators with what looked like to me, hundreds of wires and tubes attached to him. "What are all those tubes for" I asked the nurse, "to assess his vital organs, to feed him, monitor his temperature and to keep him breathing" she responded, "to keep him breathing? So he dies without having that assisting him?" I replied choking up, "he should be fine, hopefully he won't need it for too long", little man was premature by 7 weeks, so his lungs were underdeveloped, he also looked yellow which the nurse explained was because he had jaundice so there was a white light shining on him. I had seen so many spectrums of colour recently, I started to wish I was colour blind!

Looking around the room, I saw a few couples sitting beside their baby's incubators who looked distraught, some with bloodshot eyes, others looked severely tired and stressed. It quickly dawned on me, I was not in a place where there were visually delighted new parents holding babies, there are no sounds of crying new-borns, laughter, or feelings of happiness. "What room is this please nurse" I asked, "intensive care unit" she said, "pardon? Say again" "this is the intensive care unit for sick babies" she reiterated. I then went through my finely honed repertoire of intense questioning to seek the positivity needed that could enable me to calm down, but the reality was I was in a place where people die every single day. My son was fighting for his little life and without those machines he would not make it. My eyes were sore, not just from the crying, I was rubbing them as they were itching, my throat tickling and nose stuffy. I know these sensations well having suffered from allergies such as nuts, hay fever and asthma since a kid so I scanned the room seeking the enemy attacking my immune system.

In the far corner there were a mountain of flowers, most noticeably my nemesis with its attention seeking and showboating red pollen anthers, Lilies. "damn things, not like I can even go over there and cut the damn pollen out of them" I thought, my agitation quickly became solemn as I noticed there was no baby in that incubator and among the many flowers were cards, condolences cards, my eyes then gazed through the floral screen to a slender petite silhouette sitting alone with tissue in hand sobbing, that flower couldn't be a more delicate and ruthless symbol of where we were – Lily the flower of happiness and sorrow. "Daddy, I said would you like to do the honours?" the nurse said, whilst holding a sharp pair of scissors sharply regaining my focus, "do what" I said, "the umbilical cord", another first, proud dad moment. My sperm donor, known as father, wasn't around to cut my umbilical cord when I was born nor was on my birth certificate, perhaps he didn't want to claim me or he believed the bookies showing the 2:35pm at Epsom that day would be the race that changed his fortunes, a better bet than witnessing his son being born it seems. I can't even claim to be his first-born son as his roving eye would have other descendants dotted across these shores and beyond, of course, my mum, sister or I didn't know who our step relatives were which was not by coincidence but design. A Jamaican man's life and lust for women is infamous, steeped in secrecy, smoke, and mirrors, and culturally as a child you "don't ask big people questions" and you are "seen and not heard", a trait I had every intention of breaking and not modelling on my offspring.

"Is this the right place? Don't want to chop off his pride" I said. I made the incision which was filmed by one of the nurses so I could show mummy who had missed this special landmark, "how is mum" I asked, "sorry, we only deal with baby, someone will come and let you know about mummy". Sure enough, 45 minutes later a familiar nurse came in and told me "The doctors have just finished stitching mummy up from the caesarean and has just come round from the anaesthetic. She may be a bit groggy". "That's fine nurse, as long as she is alive and well" I replied, "she's definitely alive dad, don't worry about that, everything went perfect" she reassured me. She will never know how relieving and comforting those words were. The nurse then escorted me to the recovery room, where they were doing observations on her organs to ensure everything was in working order following the emergency operation. Lauren was laying on the bed, eyes closed, "sure she is ok Doc?" I asked, "Yes, go over and see her "she prompted. I ran over to her almost tripping over and pulling out all the wires she was hooked up to, "Hey baby, well done, you've done amazing. Our son is beautiful, you are incredible, I'm so proud of you", Lauren opened her eyes slowly and smiled, she then said softly "is he ok? I want to see him; I want to hold him".

CHAPTER ELEVEN

~

A Woman's Worth

Having grown up around women, I always felt like I understood them to a degree and wholly valued all the nuances, tones, and varying forms of communication I would see and hear on a daily basis that make them special and so complex. So naturally I treated all women with the utmost respect and humility, the minimum of what they deserve, as that's how I was raised.

Thankfully Lauren got the final ok from the doctors and she could now meet her son for the first time, she needed a wheelchair as a result of the caesarean birth, her stomach had been ripped open, so she was extremely sore. We followed safety protocol and waited for one of the specialist nurses to let us into the intensive care unit, used anti-bacterial gel before entering, then washed our hands when inside. I wheeled Lauren over to our son's cubicle, "first time mummy meeting baby?" yes, I replied choking up. The nurse carefully took our son out of the cubicle and placed him in Laurens arms, then manoeuvred her apron so mummy and baby could have skin to skin contact for the first time. It was at that precise moment the tears started streaming down my face, "this is your son babe, and this is our family" I whispered in her ear. This was the happiest and most emotional moment of my life.

I was taking photos and video recording to capture these priceless moments; Lauren was still very drowsy and poorly so wanted to be able to show her footage should she forget anything. As I was filming, I was looking at Lauren through a different lens, I unearthed a whole new level of profound respect and admiration for what she went through and marvelled at what a woman's body has to endure to bring life into the world. She had never looked as beautiful to me as when holding our son in her arms, I fell in love with her all over again and knew that I would do anything to protect and nurture my new family. I had a whole new 'why' to motivate and drive me.

Our families went home soon after meeting their grandson and nephew, which gave Lauren and I time to rest and reflect back in our room on what was a momentous and traumatic day in equal measure. I was showing her photos of the moment our son was born, the umbilical cord ceremony and all the different angles of our baby boy. We were then interrupted by a midwife called Sophie who had just started her shift taking over from a lovely girl called Denny, Sophie was checking Laurens Catheter. The urinary catheter was installed to empty her bladder before the surgery and to help perform tests, Sophie carefully changed it and then asked Lauren "are you producing liquid gold yet?", "sorry, producing what Sophie?" Lauren replied. Meanwhile I was wide-eyed giddy, as if we were about to strike oil. Sophie then explained that Colostrum is often described as liquid gold due to the nourishing and special properties that are so valuable to new-born babies. Oh, and its yellow colour!

"No I'm not producing any colostrum at the moment" Lauren confirmed, Sophie raised an eyebrow and said "are you sure? You should be producing it now, do you mind if I check", "sure go ahead" Lauren replied. Sophie then spent 30 seconds massaging Lauren's right breast and then squeezed the area surrounding the nipple firmly and to our pleasant surprise, Sophie struck gold! A thick buttery yellow fluid came flowing out, "see, told you, the female body knows what it has to do in order to take care of baby". She then proceeded to tell us that we would have mine this gold twice a day, morning, and evening, so that they could give it to our baby through his feeding tube as it's very easy to digest and the perfect first food for him. "So how do I capture the milk then" I said, sounding like a true Neanderthal, "with a syringe" Sophie explained, the process is called antenatal colostrum harvesting, and she outlined the steps. It was my job to collect the fluid using a 1mil syringe, ensuring hands are washed thoroughly with soap and hot water, then once collected to label the syringe with Lauren's full name, the date, and her hospital number. This is so the colostrum could be frozen and correctly assigned to our baby when needed, a new syringe would have to be used each time, Sophie then gave us a bag full of the syringes and the labels. "This is an important job daddy, your son needs this" Sophie told me assertively, I welcomed the responsibility "don't worry, I've got this" I said, immediately I put alarm reminders on my phone so that it alerted me at 9am and 7pm every day, I wasn't going to let down my son or Lauren. When Sophie left the room, I started researching colostrum and as Lauren had a nap, watched YouTube videos about it and simply couldn't believe that a woman's body could produce something so remarkable, almost supernatural. Lauren had always told me

53

that the body could produce medicine that could fight disease for babies, but I thought she was exaggerating a woman's wonders or just messing with me, she wasn't!

"Up to two-thirds of the cells in colostrum are white blood cells that guard against infections, as well as helping baby start fighting infections for himself. 1 "White blood cells are important as far as immune responses are concerned. They provide protection and challenge pathogens," explains Professor Peter Hartmann, a leading expert in the science of lactation, based at The University of Western Australia. Having left the protection of your body, your baby needs to be ready for new challenges in the world around him. The white blood cells in colostrum produce antibodies that can neutralise bacteria orviruses. These antibodies are particularly effective against tummy upsets and diarrhoea – important for young babies who have immature guts.

"Colostrum is especially rich in a crucial antibody called sIgA. This protects baby against disease, not by passing into his bloodstream, but by lining his gastrointestinal tract. Molecules that have provided an immune defence against infection in the mother are transported in her blood to the breast, join together to form sIgA, and are secreted into her colostrum," explains Professor Hartmann. "This sIgA becomes concentrated in the mucus lining of the baby's gut and respiratory system, protecting against illnesses the mother has already experienced." Colostrum is also rich in other immunologic components and growth factors that stimulate growth of protective mucus membranes in your baby's intestines. And while that's happening, the prebiotics in colostrum feed and build up the 'good' bacteria in the baby's gut.

As well as protecting against tummy upsets, colostrum acts like a laxative that makes your new-born poo frequently.

This helps empty his bowels of everything he ingested while in the womb, in the form of meconium – dark, sticky stools. Frequent pooing also reduces an infant's risk of new-born jaundice. Your baby is born with high levels of red blood cells, which take oxygen around his body. When these cells break down, his liver helps to process them, creating a by-product called bilirubin. If your baby's liver isn't developed enough to process the bilirubin, it builds up in his system, causing jaundice. The laxative properties of colostrum help your baby flush out bilirubin in his poo.

This would be vital for our son as he had new-born jaundice which placed even further significance on me keeping the flow of liquid gold consistent and on schedule. It's the carotenoids and vitamin A in colostrum that give it the distinctive yellowy colour. Vitamin A is important for a baby's vision (vitamin A deficiency is a major cause of blindness worldwide), as well as keeping his skin and immune system healthy. Babies are usually born with low reserves of vitamin A,8 so colostrum helps make up the deficit. Colostrum is rich in minerals too, such as magnesium, which supports your baby's heart and bones; and copper and zinc, which help develop his immune system. Zinc also aids brain development, and there's nearly four times more zinc in colostrum than in mature milk to support a new-born's rapidly developing brain.

It also contains numerous other components that support your baby's growth and development. Scientists are still working out the part some of them play. "Colostrum maintains the same composition until about 30 hours after birth," says Professor Hartmann. "It's relatively high in protein because all the antibodies in it are proteins. It's relatively low in lactose [the milk sugar], and the fat is a different composition to that in mature milk." And because

colostrum has a similar make-up to amniotic fluid (which your baby has been swallowing and excreting in your womb), its ideal easing for his transition to the outside world."
(https://www.medela.co.uk/breastfeeding/mums-journey/colostrum)

My mind was blown, I could not fathom how women could naturally harvest this substance so precious to babies, I would later find out through tumbling ever further down the colostrum rabbit hole that this elixir of life has been created in tablet form and is used by adults for a variety of purposes. Some athletes use it for respiratory health and increased athletic performance, it can assist in alleviating stomach issues such as bloating and is huge in popularity and usage in the health and beauty industry. Whereby Colostrum is believed to have acne-fighting bacteria that improves the skin, whilst also helps enhance hair growth and health by reducing inflammation for the scalp and fighting off bacteria.

It then dawned on me that I was in charge of extracting this serum with a tiny 1mil syringe. No pressure then!

I sat there in my blue chair staring at Lauren sleeping, absorbing everything I had just read and watched in sheer awe of her and the marvel of a woman. I reflected on all that I had learnt attending antenatal classes and hypnobirthing that detailed what the woman's body does to prepare for the birthing process and the pain Lauren had suffered unknowingly through Pre-eclampsia and HELLP syndrome, whilst navigating the perils of childbirth that still kills millions of women each year and shook my head in disbelief shedding tears. This is not even to mention the sacrifice women make when having children that has a detrimental impact on their careers, earnings, and self-identity, with an overwhelming lack of support from employers, government policy and legislation and most telling, men! Words can't even do justice do the qualities women possess, the most expensive 24 carat gold in the world doesn't come close. Women create a gold more valuable.

I now completely appreciated Lauren's worth but even more so, a woman's worth.

The value of it... Priceless!

CHAPTER TWELVE

~

Special Care

"Morni... oh so sorry to interrupt", the doctor came into our cubicle doing the morning rounds, "you should always knock first before entering a room Doc", I said in jest. He had walked in unannounced to me cupping one of Lauren's breasts and massaging the flow of colostrum into a syringe. "Its fine Dr, don't worry, good morning" Lauren said.

He came to inform us that our son had been taken off the assisted breathing machine and been moved to the special care neonatal unit because he was breathing normally by himself. Lauren and I were elated, it meant he was not in intensive care anymore and was the first progressive leap towards him coming home, our boy was breathing! He said they were just finishing setting his station up and we could pop down there in an hour's time, so Lauren and I got ourselves ready to see our son's temporary new home. We were also being moved to a new room; I asked them to transport my blue chair from upstairs down to our new fancy room with ensuite. They did offer an alternative chair but blue and I had gone through too much together and I wasn't going to cheat on it with some other old rocking chair. They kindly reunited us, and this new room would be where we stayed until Lauren was given the all clear to be discharged home.

We realised all the clothes we had purchased were for new-borns but at full term, our son was premature therefore couldn't fit into any of them. There was no way my boy was going to be looking like a 90's rapper with baggy clothes, though that oversized look has come back in fashion. I went straight out to the shops to look for premature new-born clothes, the options and range were scarce and highlighted a clear problem and gap in the market for premature babies, but I found some doable options for the time being. Online stores had more variety than in traditional stores, so I ordered a bundle to be delivered. The nurses had kindly put him in clothes that had been donated for the interim, which we were very grateful for.

"The Neonatal Unit at St Georges Hospital looks after new-born babies with a wide range of medical and surgical conditions. Many of the babies are born prematurely. The Unit is divided into 3 nurseries – Intensive Care (12 cots), High Dependency Care (9 cots), and Special Care (18 cots). Babies may be admitted to the neonatal unit if they are born at St George's Hospital, or if they are born outside of St George's but need their specialist medical or surgical services." (stgeorges.nhs.uk)

My son was in this unit because he was 7 weeks premature as a result of preeclampsia and HELLP syndrome causing an emergency C section to be performed for the safety of mother and baby. However premature babies are at heightened risk of health complications, babies born more than 3 weeks earlier than their expected due date (before the start of the 37th week of pregnancy) are called premature. Premature babies (preemies) didn't have enough time to grow and develop as much as they should have before birth, in majority of instances, doctors don't know why babies are born early.

When they do know, it's often because a mother, such as Lauren, has a health problem during pregnancy, such as;

- an infection of the amniotic membranes or vaginal or urinary tracts
- diabetes (high blood sugar)
- heart or kidney problems
- Hypertension (high blood pressure)

Babies may also be born early if:

- the mother's womb is not shaped typically
- there's bleeding, often due to a low-lying placenta (placenta previa) or a placenta that separates from the womb (placental abruption)
- they're part of a multiple birth (twins, triplets, or more)
- the mother smoked, used drugs, or drank alcohol while pregnant
- the mother was underweight before pregnancy or didn't gain enough weight during pregnancy

Premature babies, especially those born very early, often have complicated medical problems. The earlier a baby is born, the higher the risk of complications depending on how early the baby may be;

- **Late preterm,** born between 34 and 36 completed weeks of pregnancy
- **Moderately preterm,** born between 32 and 34 weeks of pregnancy
- **Very preterm,** born at less than 32 weeks of pregnancy
- **Extremely preterm,** born at or before 25 weeks of pregnancy.

Most premature births occur in the late preterm stage.

Preemies can have many special needs. Younger and smaller babies tend to have more health problems than babies born closer to their due dates." (mayoclinic.org) So they often need care in a neonatal intensive care unit (NICU) which was where our little own preemie was when he was born. Our son would have visited 2 of the 3 nurseries within his first 72 hours of life, Lauren completed the full house though, as she was being looked after in the high dependency unit. Extremely sobering, my family were not out of the woods yet, not by any means.

To enter the special care unit was like Fort Knox to enter, having to press a video buzzer and wait for someone to answer. You then have to state who you are and what baby you are here to see and your relation to baby. This is every single time, regardless of how many times you are in and out of that unit. Once inside you are instructed to use anti bacteria gel, there is an area for coats and seating zone, small kitchen, toilets and private rooms. Sleeves must be rolled up before entering the main baby room through the double doors. Washing hands thoroughly with soap is the first thing that must be done. At first, I felt quite taken aback at the sheer size of the room and the array of incubators with premature/sick babies. The smell was relaxing and created an aura of tranquility, that peace disturbed only by the welcome sound of crying babies every so often. My overarching feeling of the unit was safety, I felt my son was in a safe and secure space where he could grow, thrive and was being looked after by specialists.

As Lauren and I walked in for the first time, our son's incubator was on the far right upon entering the ward. One of the nurses then explained how things worked, where everything was and asked us to provide a list of names who were permitted to see our baby even if we were not present. The list was small but reassuring that no one could just enter and see or touch our boy if they were not permitted to. There would always be a clipboard which showed the date and time in which baby had a wet or dirty nappy, a feed and temperature check. There would be a fun poster on wall with the name of the nurse looking after him, this would change two or three times a day due to the varying working shift patterns but was always reassuring knowing what nurse was caring for our son anytime we would visit. More often than not they would greet us immediately as we walked in and update on his progress and what had happened that morning or afternoon, the attentiveness and empathy from the nurses was first class and gave is confidence that our special baby was in safe hands.

CHAPTER THIRTEEN

~

Skin To Skin

"What needs to happen in order for us to take our son home" I asked the Dr, who we managed to catch up with just as she was finishing doing the morning rounds. She explained that our baby needed to put on more weight and establish breast feeding, regulate his own temperature, unassisted breathing, jaundice treatment and an assessment on Lauren and I competence as parents to be able to care for our baby would be judged. Many people wouldn't, but I loved the fact that they would be assessing us as parents, I wasn't worried in the slightest and never doubted our commitment and enthusiasm to listen, learn and be the best mother and father to our son as possible. Personally, I thrive on challenges, competition and targets whilst giving 110% in everything I commit to, more so I like accountability. I relished the responsibility of our son needing Lauren and I, no way would we let him down, "daddy, would you like to have skin to skin with your son?" the nurse asked me. "Umm, yes please" I timidly replied, this would be another of many dad firsts.

I didn't think that dads were encouraged to skin to skin as everything I had read or heard regarding it was naturally about the importance of mothers and baby bonding as quickly as possible which is essential. I was beaming ear to ear with excitement and happiness, I wouldn't admit it to Lauren, but I was feeling left out and a little embarrassed that I was not having any element of direct influence or control over helping my boy, or a significant part to play. How wrong I would be.

Skin to skin is just as simple as it sounds: holding my son so that his bare skin is next to mine, the benefits however being anything but simple. I had begun to quickly understand that nothing is as straightforward as it sounded when it comes to the magic of pregnancy, I mean, I was still getting my head around syringing liquid gold.

Skin-skin between mothers and new-borns is indispensable. "When mothers hold their baby skin-to-skin straight after the birth, it keeps them warm whilst helping to regulate their breathing. It also keeps blood sugar at the right level, builds up immunity to infection and they can hear and feel the comforting sound of mum's heartbeat, which they know so well from their time in the womb, they will be familiar with dad's voice too. These sounds reassure them that they are ok. Skin-to-skin contact takes the baby through a natural pattern of behaviour that midwives and doctors look for in the first hour of life. It starts with that well-known sound of a baby's first cry.

When placed skin-to-skin on her mum's chest, a new-born baby will then typically follow these stages:

- relaxing and going still while listening to your heartbeat

- opening her eyes and looking at you for the first time
- moving her hands and mouth
- crawling towards your breast
- exploring your breast
- suckling for the first time"

Lauren unfortunately couldn't experience these first precious interactions with our son because she had a caesarean operation, but the maternity team made sure she got to have skin to skin with our new-born baby at the earliest possible opportunity.

The nurse would explain that skin-to-skin contact, also known as kangaroo care, is an important part of care for sick premature or low-birth-weight babies. Skin-to-skin can help low-birth-weight babies to survive by reducing the risk of infections and hypothermia, while increasing growth and breastfeeding rates and shortening hospital stays.

The nurse carefully placed him tucked into my t shirt, it was a little tight so I ripped it open like the Hulk so there was more space, and she put a little hat on him and covered us with a blanket. Father and son, he was wrapped up in my top like a pouch, "you know skin to skin is also known as Kangaroo care" Lauren said, "whatever" I laughed off, thinking she was bantering me. "No, she is telling the truth; it really is Kangaroo care" the nurse confirmed. It was apt because I immediately became his guardian and protector, I would be carrying him forever, or at least till he was 18.

"Wow" is the only word I could muster, and it was on repeat. He was delicate, small enough to fit in the palm of my hand. He laid on my chest peacefully radiating the most electrifying warmth I had ever experienced, it was like being electrocuted, my whole body was flowing with adrenaline, this was undeniable, this was unmistakable, this was nothing I had ever felt before, this was love! Never had I experienced such an overwhelming desire and devotion to protect another person like I did right now, and it was wonderful. Nothing was more important, and nothing felt as easy and uncomplicated, I was at peace and all my stresses, worries and pent-up angst were temporarily dissolving away as he lay on my chest with our heartbeats in sync and bond unbreakable, Love.

He felt vulnerable and in need, in need of time, in need of support, in need of milk to grow and in need of love. Love and support he had unconditionally, we would be with him for as long a time as needed and the milk? The milk was coming, the colostrum was still flowing and was being fed to him through the feeding tube, so he was getting exactly what he needed in his first few days of life. "Many emotional, developmental and medical benefits of skin-to-skin for premature babies last throughout childhood." (babycentre.co.uk)

So, performing skin to skin was going to be essential in not only the health of our boy but in how quickly we could take him home. I didn't mind, it felt the most natural thing in the world, and I could do it for as long as necessary, I just hoped and wished all dads experienced this because male skin to skin definitely was not one of the tips or advice given to me. In fact, it wasn't spoken about at all, not in any of the antenatal classes or hypnobirthing, definitely a taboo subject in relation to men giving skin to skin with their new-born babies and it is baffling and toxic.

This prompted me to partake in one of my favourite pastimes, jumping down another rabbit hole, as my son lay sleeping on my chest. Dads performing skin to skin are just as essential to new-borns as mums doing it, just in a different way.

Accelerates Brain Development: Skin to skin contact is a multi-sensory experience. Holding baby on Dad's skin increases the development of essential neural pathways, which accelerates brain maturation. In addition, research shows that kangarooed babies spend more time in quiet sleep, which enhances organizational patterns in the brain and decreases baby's stress responses.

Calms, Soothes & Reduces Stress: The direct connection with Dad's skin during Kangaroo Care soothes baby so much that babies' cortisol levels (stress hormone) are measurably lowered after only 20 minutes of being held skin to skin. And, remarkably, their pain is reduced when held skin to skin. As a result, babies who experience regular Kangaroo Care often cry less and appear less agitated.

Improves Quality of Sleep: Development of mature brain function in infants depends on the quality of their sleep cycling. During skin to skin, most infants fall asleep easily, and achieve what is called "Quiet Sleep", a natural deep sleep for 60 minutes or more.

Enhances Immune System: Baby's immune system is stimulated when placed skin to skin. Dad's mature immune system passes antibodies through his skin to baby. Being on Dad's skin also increases baby's skin hydration, which provides a protective barrier from harmful bacteria entering baby's skin.

Stimulates Digestion & Weight Gain: Kangaroo Care reduces cortisol and somatostatin in babies, allowing for better absorption and digestion of nutrients, while decreasing gastrointestinal problems. With a reduction of these hormones, baby's bodies preserve brown fat (the healthy fat babies are born with), helping to maintain birth weight and keep a warm body temperature. As a result, baby's body does not have to burn its own fat stores to stay warm, resulting in better weight gain. After just one hour of skin to skin, the infant's digestive system is restored to the right balance for optimal GI function.

Synchronizes Heart Rate + Breathing: Simply put, through time spent skin to skin with Dad, baby's body learns to self-regulate, resulting in a regular and stable heartbeat and breathing pattern. 75% of sporadic breathing and slow heart rate episodes are reduced through skin-to-skin contact.

The benefits for baby alone are well worth the time spent skin to skin. But what's even more remarkable is that there are benefits for Dad too:

Promotes Psychological Well-Being: As Dad sits with baby skin to skin on his chest, oxytocin (natural "feel good" hormone) levels in his body increase. With increased oxytocin levels, Dad's testosterone levels decrease. This shift in hormones creates a "relaxation and well-being" response. This aids in Dad responding with nurturing and affectionate behaviours toward baby and allowing him to better bond with baby. As Dad is more sensitive and aware of his baby's needs, he feels more tuned-in to baby, and more confident about his parenting skills. Dads are more interactive with their infants and report a stronger bond long term if they've held baby skin to skin." (nuroobaby.com)

As I lay reading, it became evident that the warm adrenaline sensation I was feeling was in fact oxytocin, which was alleviating my stress levels and making me feel more relaxed and happier. As much as our son was poorly and needed me and his mum, I needed him. I needed him in immeasurable ways many I couldn't even communicate, beyond skin to skin. He was the missing piece of a puzzle emotionally and for the first time I was truly complete, I was not being judged, I could express myself to him, be my true self. The barriers were down for him, no guard or armour of defence. No double-breasted suit to defend against perception and bias, I belonged to him emotionally, spiritually, and physically. It was liberating.

Time seemed like an unknown concept as I had lost complete track of it. I checked my phone and panicked, "babe, how long has he been laying on me? I can only do skin to skin for 60 minutes or he could overheat" I said, "it's defo not been an hour yet, should be ok" Lauren replied. No risks with me, I called the nurse over and she put him back in the incubator, I was happy as it gave me something special to look forward to tomorrow.

Two things I couldn't do for our son as a dad that mothers can when holding skin to skin, is transform into a Dyson fan. Mothers can cool or heat a baby's temperature with their breast tissue, dads can only heat which is why we are recommended to only hold baby skin to skin for sixty minutes at a time. The other thing was produce milk for baby, I can't say I was disappointed about men not being able to do that, especially with the challenges breastfeeding can cause for women and babies.

CHAPTER FOURTEEN

~

Latching For Dear Life

With all that was going on when he was born, I hadn't got the time of birth or remembered how much our son weighed, I knew it would be in what was called the Redbook which one of the nurses explained but we hadn't received yet. Thankfully though, there was an incomplete label on the incubator, but it did have those two vital details of information present. 2:55pm and 1,812 grams.

Clearly our son putting on weight was the main focus as he weighed less than a bag of sugar currently. Therefore, Lauren being able to establish breast feeding was an important milestone, but this would be determined by how quickly and efficiently our son would latch on, which I was aware many mothers struggle with, and an immense pressure and expectation on them to do so.

I was still syringing colostrum twice a day like clockwork, and actively giving it to him through the feeding tube, which was a small, soft, plastic tube placed through his nose into the stomach, this was to provide feedings and medicines into the stomach until he could receive food to mouth directly. Being 7 weeks premature, he didn't have the required strength and coordination to be able to suck or swallow well enough to bottle or breastfeed at this stage. Tube feedings allowed him to get some or all feeding into the stomach which was the most efficient and safest way to provide nutrition, we would establish what our son thought of the tube in the coming days and get a glimpse of his personality.

Lauren was insistent that she wanted to breastfeed and whilst colostrum was still flowing, it was a relief when she started to express milk. Laurens breastmilk would be tailor-made for our baby, containing "vitamins and minerals and is always available, it also offers protection from certain infections and helps improve your baby's long-term health. Breastfeeding reduces the risk of SIDS (sudden infant death syndrome),childhood diabetes and leukemia." (https://www.nhs.uk/start4life/baby/feeding-your-baby/breastfeeding/)

With Lauren producing milk, it meant my job as a liquid gold miner had come to an end. I was gutted, "Don't worry, you'll be able to syringe the milk into his feeding tube until he can latch on and establish breast feeding" Lauren said, "so that basically means I've gotten a promotion then?" I replied. "Yes babe, you've finally found what you're really good at and you're calling in life…a milkman!" she said laughing.

Lauren got given a Breast pump so she could begin expressing her milk into 100mil containers, we would then label them and put into the main fridge on her designated shelf. Her milk would then be syringed out and then fed directly into the feeding tube by the milkman, me. There was a breastfeeding room within the special care unit where mums could sit in privacy and express milk in a calming environment. This would be a place that mums would connect over a shared experience and start conversation. "Another friend made in the pumping room?" I would say to Lauren when seeing her saying hello to another new mum. I would then get a full background summary on that mum like a CRB check, a reminder of the organic openness women have, to be able to communicate and forge strong bonds and rapport almost immediately. A transparency that men could benefit from, other than the general football chat and banter talk that lacks depth or more meaningful connection to underpin the friendship and create relatability and commonality so that we don't feel that we have to go through things alone or that no one else understands.

Over the next few days, Lauren would try to get our new-born to latch on when holding skin to skin, it was a skill that needed to be learnt so she was following the step-by-step guide given in her birthing pack. It wasn't easy but she never got deterred or frustrated, was kind to herself and was not putting unneeded pressure even though both of us were distinctly aware of the need to establish breastfeeding ASAP. She knew it was only a matter of time and that positive perseverance was key, Lauren would also need a tad of experience and guidance in a similar way that Sophie helped us strike gold!

"Learn from those who have walked the path before you", my mum would always tell me this when guiding me on the importance of respecting my elders and listen to valuable wisdom. One of the nurses Sunita could see our son was struggling to latch on but also that Lauren understandably was being gentle and thoughtful with how she was handling our delicate boy. Sunita had never looked after our son

72

before, but we had seen her from time to time tending to other babies in the unit. She had four kids and grew up in a big Indian family, culturally the parents look after the children then those children when older take care of the parents in old age, so there is a lifetime of knowledge that gets passed down through ancestry and generations. Sunita approached Lauren with a welcoming smile and asked, "do you mind if I help?" before either could answer, she proceeded to grab Lauren's breast, tilted our sons head and stuff the nipple into our son's mouth with such G force that I was sure there was a danger of smothering. I was expecting something with more finesse, but I guess sometimes the best results are by force. He still didn't latch on fully but there was definitely more of an attempt at suction from this more astute technique which was development and gave Lauren even more confidence.

"Will you both be doing anything nice to see the New Year in?" asked our midwife, we hadn't realised was New Year's Eve was the next day, our son would be 5 days old. The midwife continued, "I'm pleased to say that subject to the final ok from Dr Polly, you will be getting discharged from hospital tomorrow morning and going home mummy". Lauren started crying, she could actually sleep in her own bed and have a relaxing hot bath. I started getting our things together in readiness of our pending departure the next day, we then took a walk down to see our king before bedtime, when we arrived, he was crying and had milk coming out of his nose and mouth. Lauren and I were in a distressed panic, "what's happening, is he ok" we said in unison, don't worry, it's just reflux" the nurse said. "What the hell is reflex? Is he having a seizure?" I shouted, the nurse would ask us to calm down and have a seat so she could explain that reflux was completely normal, once seated she clarified that reflux is when a baby brings up milk, or is sick, during or shortly after feeding. It's very common and usually gets better on its own. Nonetheless it was a scary sight that we didn't ever want to see again but we would and many times more.

It was New Year's Eve and Dr Polly came to see us first thing in morning to confirm Lauren could go home, they had been doing regular Obs on her throughout the week and her stitches from the caesarean were heeling nicely. she gave us a kit full of needles that I had to inject into her leg or bum twice a day to prevent infection, when we opened it, the needles resembled spears, they were huge and more akin to tranquilisers given to animals.

I booked us a lovely NYE dinner at Chez Bruce which was a Michelin star restaurant located on Wandsworth common, not far from Laurens mums house and importantly the hospital. We had a lovely meal, and it was nice to share some normality with one another, but it didn't feel right, we wanted to see in the New Year with our baby boy. So, we left the restaurant early, popped into the local corner shop and purchased chocolates and Bailey's liqueur for the hardworking nurses who would be looking after all the babies in the neonatal special care unit on NYE.

We arrived at 11:30pm, "Hi mummy and daddy, your little man has been having quite the battle with his feeding tube. I have just put it back in again for the 7th time tonight which is a record for the unit" said the nurse, "he really doesn't like it and is very persistent, so we have had to put mitts on his hands". We looked into his incubator, and he had wool mitts wrapped around both hands to stop him pulling the tube out. Lauren and I couldn't stop laughing, in fact we hadn't laughed that hard for what felt like weeks, pure joy and happiness. It was the perfect way for us to see in the New Year, our little family together.

Tube gate would become legend, his antics infamous, every nurse on shift tending to him would relay the same story of him pulling out his feeding tube. He was showing his character, just weeks old. Fortitude and perseverance, it showed us that if he didn't like something he wouldn't just accept it, my mind explored to all the careers and possibilities that were at his fingertips with those qualities and traits, from a sporting superstar to astronaut. When nurses would relay his escapades, I had nothing but pride and admiration for what he was showcasing, I loved it. He was not passive but proactive and wouldn't stop until he got what he wanted; he broke his own nightly record twice more.

Unsurprisingly it wasn't long before he was establishing breastfeeding and latching onto Laurens breasts for dear life, I questioned how we would ever get him off!

CHAPTER FIFTEEN

~

Candid Canteen Conversations

Second floor, through the yellow ward, just before the turn right to the Special Care unit, was my brief safe haven on the left opposite the lifts. The canteen.

This culinary sanctuary offered me some kind of respite, solace, and serenity from what mostly felt like chaos. A brief moment to sit down with a hot meal, cup of tea and watch the news to catch up on what was going on in the world. I was in a bubble, completely out of touch with anything that didn't involve my son, Lauren, or the hospital.

Brenda was a lovely lady, big personality with a heart to match. She would greet everyone with a big smile and make them feel welcome, she was from Jamaica, where my family were from, and she could have been one of my aunts. It certainly felt it, especially the way she would bless my plate with piling up as much food as possible, then saying "Is that enough baby? "Yes Aunty, thank you", I would reply. In black culture love is shown through food, it's nostalgic, linked to music, house parties, BBQs, and specific times of the year. Brenda without realising it made me feel safe and at home, she was strict too, I had to eat all my vegetables, or I wouldn't get any sponge cake and custard for dessert.

I would pop into the canteen most evenings, depending on what time I got to the hospital from work. I would often bump into a few of the dads whose babies were also in the special care unit. There was Dave, Emmanuel, and Rob, we were all from different backgrounds and walks of life, ordinarily we probably all wouldn't be friends, but we all shared one thing in common. We were new dads whose babies were fighting against the odds in the IC3 ward, and the canteen offered us a place where we could grab a coffee and chat candidly as fathers and as men.

This was Dave's third child, so he often assumed the role of teacher, passing on his knowledge and experience which Emmanuel and I soaked up like a sponge. Felt like we were getting cheat codes to fatherhood and how to find and implement parental loopholes, his 'sleeping giant' routine of pretending to be asleep at night when the baby cries so he didn't have to do bottle feeds despite being shoved and kicked was both hilarious and distinctly narcissistic in equal measure. We would later find out Dave was a tax avoidance lawyer, which would explain his forensic and meticulous approach to parenting. Rob always seemed a little withdrawn and distant, when topics of co-parenting would be spoken about, the reason for this would come to the fore in one of our many discussions about the lack of male inclusion in the pregnancy process.

Emmanuel, a school teacher from Ghana was a very calm, polite man and a first-time dad like myself. Though mild mannered he would often get expressive and vocal when speaking passionately about how "underprepared" he was for the birth of his daughter. Highlighting the "emasculating experience through the pregnancy process that makes men feel like they are not needed and simply a spare part to do the token gestures like time keeping or preparing the birthing bag". We would all nod and "Mmm" in complete agreement having had similar feelings. This is where the often-quiet Rob would tell us his story. He was a young dad, 19, grew up in council estate and dropped out of school aged 16, but had trained as a plumber and electrician and set up his own business recently. He and the mother of his son were not together, and they didn't plan the pregnancy, they were casually dating and using contraception but as we know, it's not 100%, he confessed that he didn't want to have the baby as they were not in a committed relationship. He also felt they were too young and had many years to have children, but she was firm in her conviction that she was having it with or without him. I asked him "how do you feel about it" he said "obviously I'm elated my son is here and I love him to bits, but I had no say in the decision and it's all about the mum init" I asked him to elaborate, "We aren't needed are we? He replied, "I missed loads of the classes, no point going to them, it's just about the mum. They didn't ask me how I felt or if I needed any advice or counselling. Dads are not needed, my dad weren't around growing up, my mum raised me and my two other brothers. Kids need their mums, as men we just need sort out the money and stuff".

I felt sick to my stomach but completely understood how and why he would feel this way, especially as he had never seen his parents together and what that dynamic looks and feels like so how could he possibly see the value of what a man can bring to the family from an emotional and physically present perspective and experience? I know I couldn't. "Alright fellas, I better head off, see you man soon yeh" Rob then left the canteen, I really hoped we would see him soon as this candid conversation was an example of what men need. The platform to speak unapologetically about our truth from a male perspective and our feelings, with the support of fellow males in similar positions in a safe   non-judgemental   space.

CHAPTER SIXTEEN

~

Y Gender Reveal?

There appears to be a lack of why when it comes to Y!

Much like a baby gender reveal, where a balloon or other object is excitedly uncovered, revealing a colour symbolic of the sex of baby to be, typically blue for boy or pink for girl. Y is the chromosome that represents the male gender and as men we need to start stripping away the layers of toxic masculinity and start revealing ourselves through communication. Communicating our emotions, feelings, worries, stress, fears and anything else that is holding us back from being the best version of ourselves and providing a more open understanding of what we are thinking and feeling to our loved ones and being present.

Robs words in the canteen really resonated with me as I had friends that experienced similar anecdotes either directly or through others.

There has to be a system in place that supports first time fathers in particular and encourages inclusion and male importance to the whole pregnancy process to keep men invested in the birthing experience and accountable for raising their children, education is key to this. Like myself, boys growing up with no father have no male role model to learn from therefore the teaching has to come from other male mentors to nurture and guide young men to explain and show how pivotal they are in the futures of their offspring. This is a constant candid topic my male friends and I have, many of us having shared experiences of absent fathers, but also as young dads and men dealing with our paternal mental health.

Men are three times likely to commit suicide than women (2020 data – Samaritans.org) and there is most certainly still a taboo when it comes to male mental health, communication and opening up about feelings and emotion. Some of the similarities are striking with both traumatising factors, male suicide, and absent fathers, sharing some traits stemming from men feeling like they are a burden, not needed, or loved ones better off without them being around. These are only a few of the factors I have seen first-hand and being frustratingly unaware that my friends were even going through hard times, due to an engrained reluctance from us as men to communicate, speak out, show vulnerability, or ask for help.

There are often high stress factors impacting mental health in the background causing depression, embarrassment, guilt and lack of self-esteem, male suicide has seen a significant rise year on year but more prominently in the last few years. This rising trajectory is in parallel with the growth and increased prominence of social media, with people showing off how "great" their life is and getting instant gratification and validation from likes and comments which of course is unrealistic and hollow. I feel the more our day to day lives are centred around data, technology and thus social media, the increased likelihood these terrible stats will continue to soar, due to the pressures of false expectations these platforms perpetuate that impact how people feel about themselves and can't keep up with these mythical standards and expectations. People are rarely ever snapping or posting things that are going wrong or appear ugly in their life which would at least demonstrate some balance or redemption which would be an influential neutraliser.

One of the oxymoron's of social media platforms like twitter is freedom of speech and forums for open debate. Which promote both positive and negative views, messages of hate but also love. However can be a hostile space of trolling, bullying and critique which can be toxic and can definitely impact mental health in a harmful way. Twitter is the only social media platform I actively use in my spare time; I like to get up to date news and engage in football banter with friends and strangers. Whilst also participating in topical debates through my network of friends but also forums that bring forth conversations that don't get enough attention or spotlight in mainstream media such as fatherhood or voices and opinions from varying ethnic minority groups.

A lot of absent fathers are proactively absent through conscious behaviour, but there are also many other fathers not involved who desperately would like to be, unfortunately some dads are restricted from seeing their children for a multitude of reasons. So the topic is multi layered, but in situations where the health and safety of mother and baby is not at risk, there has to be greater support provided so that willing dads who want to be present in children lives are allowed to do so. As this is just another "easy" way for fathers to walk away and fall through the net to the detriment of the children who suffer and ultimately need their dads the most. Economic or employment status should not restrict access of willing fathers from seeing or being involved in their children's lives, these two factors I have seen first-hand negatively impact a fathers access to his offspring, despite him being able to provide other non-tangible valuables such as time, love, and support.

There are millions of amazing single mothers all around the world, just like mine, who do stellar jobs raising their children against all the odds without economic, emotional, physical or time support from the fathers, but in spite of not spite, still give those men countless opportunities to be present and active in the child's lives and those men continually disappoint, disrespect and be shown to be selfish and spineless, I speak from experience because my dad was one of those cowardly selfish men. In those situations, mothers have to protect the hearts and minds of their children and rightfully do what's in their best interests as the sole responsible, stable, and loving parent. Not visible, but the child will undoubtedly carry scars that lay beneath the surface and there will be lasting damage done, it's just to what degree and in what form it manifests itself in.

These are the nature of conversations I have with friends that often spill over to debate on social media. Community, culture, political commentator, and DJ extraordinaire, Funk Butcher, who mixed many a soundtrack to my life during my raving years, was now also mixing narratives and provoking thought on fundamental issues impacting communities and cultures with his influential platform and crucially, his male voice. He often engages in the same spaces as I do and made some important and insightful recommendations on how young fathers could be better supported whom don't necessarily have a support network around them or just need other tools they could access.

He said, "Imagine there was a podcast for young dads to watch/listen to, which would advise them on navigating fatherhood from the perspective of older fathers to help break down old tropes. Fatherhood and mental health, fatherhood and finance, fatherhood and co-parenting, fatherhood and career, fatherhood and toxic masculinity, fatherhood and relationships, fatherhood and parenting ideology are just some of the many topics that could be available and valuable to young dads.

Because whichever way we check it. Most of our decisions as dads are shaped by how it impacts our ability to do our fathering duties. So fatherhood is pretty much central to everything really. It's the reason why I say "yes" or "no" to people or opportunities. I think the point is there to be some sort of resource for young dads in there early 20's to manage the overwhelming stress of their new role as a dad. Just an audio manual to help get them through, we all could have done with one I think." (Funk Butcher) I know I most certainly could have benefitted as would have Rob, especially from older fathers who looked like me due to the cultural dialect which would make the experience more authentic and bring a better understanding and connection. This is applicable to all ethnic groups, having audio podcasts or mentors from similar cultural backgrounds would enhance and improve the overall value to what is a much-needed tool and structure for young dads.

I would take this brilliant idea which definitely should be implemented a step further and challenge the antenatal system to restructure how pregnancy classes/programmes are set up. I completely appreciate there is assistance given to fathers who need to speak to someone which of course is valuable. However I feel there needs to be a section within these standard classes where the focus is on dads and it's a safe space for dads to openly vent or give an insight into how they feel. Especially powerful in the presence of the pregnant partner as she may not be aware of how the dad to be is feeling or what concerns he may have that have nothing to do with the actual birthing process. I know that I didn't tell Lauren half of what I was going through or dealing with as I didn't want to add any additional stress or worry on her, given she had enough on her plate being pregnant with our baby. The issue with that is the angst and stress manifests itself in other ways, being short tempered and on edge, my tone and temperament changing without me realising it and feeling the weight of the world firmly on my neck and trapped because I felt I couldn't communicate how I was feeling.

How many other dads do the same thing and bottle in their fears or stresses to ensure their partners are not burdened? This is what unfortunately a lot of men do, and it is toxic and needs to change. However, the system needs to promote this change by putting a programme in place for men to feel empowered to communicate and speak openly without judgement or guilt. How many Robs are out there that run away from their responsibilities which outwardly look cowardly and selfish but with little understanding of why and the lack of important structures in place that could maybe help prevent that outcome? Or perhaps unearth nuance or complexities that may need further or specialist intervention which could ultimately keep a family unit in place and dads around. We need to do better at keeping dads present, needed, engaged, and supported. Most importantly, keep men talking!

After our last candid conversation we didn't see Rob around as much, just hoped we would in the coming days and weeks, because his premature baby and mother desperately needed him.

CHAPTER SEVENTEEN

~

What's in a name?

"What's in a name? That which we call a rose. By any other name would smell as sweet" William Shakespeare, Romeo and Juliet.

This quote from William Shakespeare suggests that external labels or titles given to you do not change your true essence, a name doesn't define who you are or what you are. It's just a word, right?

I wanted the name of my son to be embodiment of who he is, to give him strength, spirit, courage, and power to attack life without fear and be his own man. Being a man of afro Caribbean descent, and my experience as a black man, you quickly understand the power and influence words can have, many unfortunately used to demean, oppress, hurt, and limit the potential and opportunities afforded to us as black people. We see subtle and non-subtle biased played out every day which is magnified through a racial prejudiced lens in some mainstream media, through language and forced narratives that are shown that unfortunately perpetuate stereotypes and stigmas that influence and harm the way we are perceived and treated.

Despite what Shakespeare says, names and labels do indeed define people on a subconscious level and/or how others perceive them, simply because some names have too much history, and/or meaning entwined around them, or associations based on prejudice and discrimination. Consciously, I knew I didn't want to give my son an African or typically black or "culturally ethnic" name, because I have seen first-hand how particular names are perceived and how people from ethnic minority groups are negatively treated based on a name. In my working career I have seen CV's come through with an Arabic or African name and on many instances they are discarded in the bin, "wouldn't suit our target market or clientele" would often be the excuse, sometimes more blatant and disgusting racist remarks were made without the courtesy of even looking at the merits of the individual on the curriculum vitae, let alone dare afford the candidate the opportunity to actually sit in front of them and speak. Whilst it shouldn't, these experiences meant I didn't want my child to go through life having opportunities taken away and doors slammed shut based simply on the origins of a name. I also felt guilty that I was letting ignorant people impact my life choices but understanding the world is not fair and as a parent wanting to limit the threats my child is exposed to. I shouldn't have to think like this!

Everyone seemed to have an opinion on his name, our parents didn't like it, it didn't matter. One of my favourite generic captions of advice was "don't make a choice on name until you see the baby", my response "babies features change very quickly, so I think I'll take my chance on my baby growing into their name". A friend once said to me "don't seek council from family or friends about potential baby names because everyone has a story to tell about a particular person they knew who shared the same name, the choice is yours so do as you want". This was so true and the best baby advice I received, any test names we threw out there seemed to be disapproved of with tales of a stalker, weirdo, local bike or other wrong'un they knew with the same name. Creative input quickly became tiresome, so we kept our baby name thoughts to ourselves.

The label attached to the incubator detailed important information about baby, it lists mum and dads name, hospital number, gestation, delivery date, delivery time, consultant, and weight. Most importantly of course, baby name, they got his first name correct but put his mums last name on the label as opposed to my last name which would be the standard and traditional protocol being that I am his father. "What is in a name", "how could they get that wrong" I asked Lauren, "it's not like they don't see me here, I basically live in this damn hospital, I am here every single day seeing my son", I was proper annoyed, "its ok babe" Lauren said, "it's only a label, you are his dad". Of course, she was right, practically speaking, however I saw my last name being absent from that label as an act of violence and insinuation that I am absent, not important, and not needed. I couldn't possibly fathom such an error was a simple mistake, I am claiming my son, what my dad didn't do for me, and I am proud to be his dad.

As much as I am nothing like my own dad, my experiences without him in my life definitely shape my overwhelming desire to ensure that I am not perceived to share any of his traits, and this enforces my insecure need to be seen outwardly as a loving and ever-present dad. Not a "baby daddy", "waste man dad" or any other term reflecting a man not fulfilling his parental duty. This is not, and will not be me and I proudly hold that chip on my shoulder, in my case, an apple most certainly does NOT fall far from the tree!

By DNA he was our dad but ironically, he wasn't even that on paper, let alone actions, he was not present for my birth nor on my birth certificate and despite my mum trying for much of my adolescent years to get him to sign documents so my sister and I could have his last name, he wouldn't. Nor did we want to take his name, "it is the done thing" my mum would often say, followed by "I don't want people to think you are bastards with no father". As always, mum was unselfishly trying to do what she felt was best for us, but she would continually overestimate the importance of his name and devalue her role in being both parents and the immense strength, pride and value my sister and I acquired from carrying her last name. We wear it like a badge of honour, and it encapsulates who we are and that is irreplaceable.

"What is in a name?" an awful bloody lot.

CHAPTER EIGHTEEN

~

Melanin

As I rolled my sleeves up and began washing my hands in the sink by the incubator, I noticed a new item on the baby station, among the cotton wool that we used to clean his bum from the milky wet poos, thermometer, baby grows and feeding syringes was a bright red book. I picked it up, Lauren was sitting in the chair expressing milk with the pump, "what's this book" I said, "it's called the red book, I literally have just seen it too, they must have put it there when I went to get the express pump" Lauren replied.

The Red Book contains your baby's details and information about the growth and development of your baby– it's where measurements are recorded, and immunisations are detailed. Health Visitors and Doctors review this information, so you bring the Red Book to any medical appointments attended.

Lauren got up to put her freshly pumped milk into her section of the fridge, so after saying hello to my son and telling him about my day, I sat in the chair and flicked through the red book. Just as I was getting over name-gate where my last name was omitted, a whole new situation would spark even deeper feelings regarding race, racial bias, and unconscious bias. Under the personal information section, there was a heading labelled "ethnicity" beside this the hospital had put my son, who is mixed race, ethnicity as White! I was stunned, "no fucking way" I said out loud, so not only did they fail to give my son my last name, but they also now referred to his ethnicity as "white". I mean, did the nurses and doctors not see me or value my worth as a black man and human being? It's bad enough black history is whitewashed, but whitewash my son? No way was I accepting this, I was absolutely livid and ready to explode, were they purposely doing these "subtle errors" to gaslight me so that I get aggressive and live up to the angry black man false narrative? Lauren arrived back and immediately sensed I was agitated, "what's wrong" she said, "They have labelled our son's ethnicity as white that is what's wrong". She was equally shocked and angry, "how could they do that, just because he is fair skinned? They see you here all the time", I was so hurt and offended, this is exactly the implicit bias I had experienced throughout my life, a shared familiarity among all black people, it's not aggressive and direct but in some ways more impactful as it comes from a deep-rooted belief system that makes the person feel they are not doing anything wrong, its engrained.

Like my son, my dad was mixed race, had fair skin, curly hair, grey eyes. His mother was Cherokee Indian and dad Scottish white, I took more of my mum's physical features, but have my dad's height and unmistakeable forehead. My son clearly has taken similar traits from my dad, but it would be impossible for the nurses to distinguish with certainty the ethnicity of a two-month premature baby who is jaundice without seeing both parents. To then compound that lazy assumption by documenting it formally in the Redbook that would follow my child's health journey throughout early life was deplorable.

Throughout our relationship Lauren and I would often discuss race when situations would occur in the world or just my experiences being a black man. During her pregnancy, these conversations would occur more frequently because it is not something she ever had to think about, being white. However, we were going to be having a bi-racial child in a country and world where institutional racism exists, and our child would have to navigate and deal with discrimination and potential self-identity issues as a result of discrimination. These discussions would sometimes get extremely heated because Lauren would on occasions sound ignorant or be dismissive because she couldn't fathom certain issues being attributed to race due to her not having experienced it. Thankfully, but as the world began focusing on injustices taking place with police brutality, and the spotlight firmly on race, it opened her eyes on micro aggressions involving attitudes and stereotypes that had affected her thinking. She then began to educate herself and started having difficult conversations with her black friends and my family, whilst reading books such as, Natives, by acclaimed writer, musician and historian, Akala.

I've seen biracial friends struggle growing up with identity issues, not feeling quite black enough for black friends or white enough for white friends. With very light skin, can often find that those people are exposed to even more indirect racism as they don't "look" black so are subjected to hearing or seeing racism in front of them with the perpetrators unaware of their black origins. This can be a lonely place which can result in isolation and internalised racism which is truly disturbing. It occurs when the racial or ethnic group being discriminated against begins to accept society's racist attitudes and beliefs. In other words, the so called 'inferiority' of one's own ethnic or racial group is believed. For example, that black people are not as intelligent as white people, and we see this perpetuated false ideology institutionalised in the education system and police force. Too also in the black community itself, till this day there is a false belief that lighter skinned people are more attractive than darker skinned which has caused much harm to black women especially, when looking at how they are represented in the media and the creative arts, where they are hugely underrepresented with lighter skinned deemed the more palatable.

In the Caribbean there are still alarming problems, with black people bleaching their skin to appear lighter which in my eyes is the most depressing example of internalised racism evident in present day. This form of racism is descendant from slavery where fairer skinned slaves would get better treatment from the slave masters who purposely pit black people against one another. Growing up in South East London, at school, light skinned girls and boys were deemed a "lighty" and more sought after amongst the opposite sex, they were also adored in music videos and greater represented in media and visual platforms. Dark skinned people were deemed less desirable and called "darkie", "blick" or other terms that referred to the larger amounts of melanin in their skin. This created a sense of privilege to lighter skinned people and resulted in division among black people.

Lauren and I speak about what form of racism our son will be faced with due to his fair skin tone. I believe the most common will be in the micro aggressions form, with damaging attitudes, behaviours, humiliations, and jokes that people from minority groups face on a daily basis. Racial micro aggressions have been described as 'the new face of racism' (Sue, et al, 2007). Due to the tone of his skin, he will, without conscious choice, be in the presence of racism or with those unaware of his ethic background as they assume he could be white. Just like the hospital did when labelling his ethnicity as white, unfortunately this discrimination will be a theme and he will have to justify his blackness and defend his ethnicity. Which will be emotionally draining and disappointing especially if it is people, he deems friends or people in positions of authority. He will lose friends. Conversely, he will receive favourable compliments based on his features much like what I saw growing up which could give him a sense of entitlement that boosts his self-esteem and makes him feel he is more desirable and better than other black people. Only guidance and education will prevent this, as the question of how did we as black people, acquire lighter skin? Unearths truths that once understood would prevent any belief or notion that the melanin in your skin makes you more valuable than any other human being, let alone ethic group.

It's very important that as his father I teach and focus on the education of black history which only gets spotlight a month a year within the school curriculum. The system is not designed to focus on all black history therefore children of ethnic minorities are made to feel only white people did incredible things because that is what they are being taught. This in my opinion is what increases and enhances racial bias in the UK, there is no acknowledgement of the bad that Britain has done. Ironically, no ownership, something they should come second nature as Great Britain were the pioneers of the slave trade and fought vehemently for it to continue. Brittana rules the world has a completely different melody to people from ethnic backgrounds.

Especially those colonised by Britain, like the Caribbean islands who fought in world wars for Britain, help rebuild the country and came to aid when labour was needed. Black War heroes have never been properly recognised and acknowledged and the treatment of the Windrush generation is nothing short of disgraceful. These types of annotates are whitewashed from the history being taught in this country, maybe if it was there would be better balanced children not growing up believing Britain is better than everyone else more composed understanding and well-rounded worldly view.

Knowledge is power and the more he knows the more empowered and respected, he will be when he speaks on black history and more importantly, he will be confident. Confident among all races to speak his truth and be confident in his own skin. This is my responsibility and duty as his father, to instil immense pride and unwavering confidence for him to be proud about his background and defend it. To know that black women and men have done extraordinary things for the world despite oppression and not just in sport, where the majority of our achievements are lauded. But we have changed the world in science, engineering, mathematics, civil and political rights, invention, fashion, music and much of what the world knows and enjoys that have come from black origins, this must be learnt and celebrated so he knows he can do and be whatever he wants to. Anything is possible and hopefully as he grows up, he won't have to work twice as hard, and the world will mature too and take greater leaps of progressive change so his generation "will not be judged by the colour of their skin, but by the content of their character." Martin Luther King, Jr.

I pray it's not just a dream...

CHAPTER NINETEEN

~

Paternal Health

"Your back at work next week babe, how do you feel"
Lauren asked, "yes fine, not ideal but I'll just get on with it"
I replied, in reality I immediately felt a weight heavy on my
neck and my mind began racing about things I needed to
organise in the office and get my team firing on all
cylinders, and as a leader that energy and direction had to
come from me leading by example. But I wasn't ready, I
knew I wasn't but what could I do? There is no quitting in
me, and I had to step up and just get on with it and produce
results, regardless of the life changing events that were
happening in my life.

As my thoughts began to transition into focused work
mode, I was feeling more and more anxiety and on edge. It
also dawned on me that I hadn't told anyone outside my
immediate family about the birth of my child. Family
relatives, close friends and friends, colleagues and my boss
were all left in the dark. I mean, is that normal? Friends in

my WhatsApp groups were now concerned by my lack of participation and were messaging privately if "everything ok bro, you been mad quiet in the group. Everything good?" I would read it and come out of the app.

This was self-preservation; I couldn't possibly bear vocalising to other people what was happening and having to field their concerns and have them fuss. Worse yet, should the unthinkable happen I would have to deliver heart-breaking news. This coping mechanism undoubtedly stems from my childhood where I couldn't get excited about things in fear they didn't happen. The disappointment too disappointing, too many times waiting for dad to take me somewhere and then he not show up, or promising me things that would never arrive, or trips abroad that didn't happen. It's plagued the way I communicate and how I react to things, I struggle to show that I am excited about something or truly happy in case something goes wrong, this has on occasions negatively impacted loved ones or people around me where I can appear aloof or subdued in moments of celebration. But only when it involves me, other people I'm the first one to laud success or be the life and soul of party for that other person celebrating, just not myself. How could I possibly tell people my child was born 7 weeks early and was in intensive care, what if he didn't make it? I couldn't fathom opening myself up in a state of complete vulnerability and sharing the biggest experience of my life with them whilst the outcome was still uncertain.

I struggle to show emotion and can come across as non-empathetic and cold on an emotional level, where the perception is that I don't care for or need anyone, a closed book. This insightful, self-aware, and emotionally intelligent assessment I wish was from self-development of my working on myself, instead was consistent feedback from people throughout my life who dared get close enough to me but still cared enough to tell me. The reality couldn't be further from the truth, but I protect my heart and myself from people, not wanting to give any power to others that could come back to hurt me. My trust in people is even more fragile and I can cut people off without a second thought, but what I lack in verbal communication I make up for with action, I show my love and consideration through thoughtful gestures, loyalty and being consistent. My word is my bond, if I say I'm going to do something I do it, just wish those you supposedly know me would understand that.

The property market was booming, demand soaring as a result of the stability caused by Britain finally leaving the EU after what was a controversial Brexit vote that divided the country. The government securing a trade deal with the EU added further solidity, because political and economic factors directly influence markets, and the housing market is no different and is built on consumer confidence. Those macro factors directly affect the buoyancy of purchasers and vendors wanting to buy and sell respectively. I had felt this surge of optimism before, the pace and frenzy were like being reunited with an old friend, familiar face. The pulse of the market felt like the beginning of the boom years of 2007, 2014 and 2015 prior to global recession, financial banking crisis, general elections, snap elections, or Brexit. Confidence was high, pent up demand and momentum causing property prices to increase and my KPI's and targets were being smashed, performance up 20% on prior year whilst mirroring record-breaking trading periods of yesteryear and I had dominant market share ahead of the competition. Work was going well.

My flat sale however was having major issues due to the development having the similar composition of cladding that caused the horrific Grenfell tower catastrophe, as a result I couldn't complete on the purchase of the house I was trying to buy as I needed the proceeds from the sale. my promotion to a new role was going well but the volume of activity was triple the demands of my previous role which wasn't made any easier by the fact that I was severely short-staffed which only exasperated my hectic workload. Then of course I had my beautiful new-born son in the special care unit and was still coming to terms with the turbulent nature of his arrival and ongoing worries. House buying and selling, new job and baby - one of those stress factors would be challenging enough, but all 4 at once? I was at breaking point, but I didn't know it.

My day would start at 6am, getting into work early to get a head start before my team came in and the bell rang for trading to begin for the day. I would power through the day with high intensity then head straight to the hospital after work for 8pm, then spend as long with my son and Lauren as possible then either crash at Laurens mums house or travel back home to bed circa 12am. Then I was up at 6am to do it all over again, this was the cycle. I would sometimes manage to actually eat a meal if I managed to arrive at the hospital a little earlier than expected, I would pit stop at the canteen for a quick refuel from Brenda.

I bumped into Emmanuel and Dave a few times in the canteen, sometimes we would be in the special care unit and give one another 'the look' to say, "meet you in the canteen in 5 mins". We would then offer our partners a coffee or sweet treat to boost their energy levels and then run off together to play like little kids. We hadn't seen Rob for a while now, Lauren would later find out, through pump room chat with his daughter's mum that he had become more and more withdrawn and hadn't been to see his daughter in the last three weeks. I was gutted, we didn't get through to him nor did we have enough opportunity to have more of our candid canteen conversations that might have kept him more engaged or at the very least gave him a support system to turn to, a brotherhood or more apt, a fatherhood.

This news gave me a sudden jolt, I hadn't been communicating in the way I was hoping Rob would, I was isolating myself from friends and family and then basically blaming them for not understanding what I was going through yet I wasn't communicating with anyone as to how I was feeling and the heavy stress factors weighing heavy on my mind.

I was drained, I felt mentally trapped but all I know is to keep going and keep pushing. That's all I saw my mum ever do, suck it up and keep going. I would pretend disappointment didn't happen and compartmentalize far far away in the abyss of my brain, no good could come of dwelling on upsetting things, strive forward, focus on positives and what I can do control and impact, that is my mentality. I can work harder than anyone else and I almost saw it my current situation as a competition with myself. Could I manage all these events at the same time without showing fragility and still excel at work to a high level whilst making it look effortlessly easy like a swan? I could...but at what cost?

My mum was noticing changes in me that I couldn't even see, I was becoming very snappy and short tempered, I was tired. "Are you ok, you can tell me anything you know" she would say, "I'm fine" is how I would always respond. Exactly how I have been all my life, I will just get through it on my own without help, my sister Lisa is a fully qualified counsellor and even with her specialist expertise, she couldn't break down my toxic wall of silence and get through to me in any meaningful way.

Both her and my mum, had seen that I was beginning to stutter more frequently, something I had done ever since a child, the cause? Unknown, Jamaican myth says it's because my uncle Earl had cut my hair before I could say my first words when we had a rare family holiday to Jamaica. I just remember the anxiety and fear I felt when I was 6 years old, sitting at the top of the stairs, watching my dad argue with my mum after he came home drunk, and wanting to scream at him and help my mum but no words were coming out my mouth. That feeling of being trapped, voiceless, powerless, and unable to move to protect my mother still haunts me to this day, which in no small part is why I attack things head on the way I do with no handbrake on or restraint. But the consequence of that experience is what I believe to be the underlining trauma that caused the anxiety and panic when speaking resulting in the stammer.

I know how to not stutter, having learned techniques when in speech therapy as a child that involves controlling my breathing, slowing down when speaking, and thinking about what I am going to say before saying it. These skills helped me a lot but thinking so much can be mentally draining, especially when tired. Having to continually figure out what words to use in place of ones that I know will trip me up based on a tricky syllable means my mind is constantly working at high speed and can cause apprehension especially when speaking in front of large people or strangers I don't know. When fatigued, that sense of panic to get what I need to say out, to avoid that awkward period of silence while people wait patiently for me to get my words out, feels suffocating. One positive though, I had become a human thesaurus, learning a variety of different words with the same meaning to try and stop myself verbally tripping up…fair to say that I am awesome at scrabble!

CHAPTER TWENTY

~

Bloodline

I've seen friend's open doors where family have only closed them...

How do you turn away a mother and two young children in need, who turn up at your front door in middle of night seeking refuge and shut the door on them? This was family, blood relatives. If blood is supposed to be thicker than water then give me a 1.5 litre bottle of Evian water instead, still not sparkling, because there is nothing bubbly or exciting about experiences like that and it negatively impacted my ability to trust people or ask anyone for help! 90% of blood is made up of water, and the human body is 60% water so metaphorically I could survive without those type of blood streams in my life, H20 much more purifying, a necessity, simple and what I valued most, transparent.

Excluding Family residing across the pond aside, friends

on these shores have always shown us the greatest kindness and opened their homes to us – Marlene & Bertie opened their door to us that night and have been true family which we will never forget. Then there's Aunty Peggy, who used to work with my mother, she was white and unrelated to us, but we called her aunty out of respect. I would see her sometimes only once or twice a year, but she would sit with me, encourage me and always tell my mum how smart I was, even when the primary school scores said different, she saw something in me. She would prepare her specialty for us whenever we visited, toad in the hole, I used to love it, and as we were leaving, she would always secretly give me a pound coin or note to buy some sweets and never would a birthday go by without a card from her with money either falling or floating from the middle of it. I couldn't even get that amount of value from my own dad, not the money but the belief and worth Aunt Peggy had in me. Noteworthy.

"What's happened to my positive, smart, and handsome son with the big infectious smile? I am worried about you Paul", my mum said, followed by "Your son and Lauren need you, don't be a slave to work because if you drop dead they will replace you in a month", she wasn't wrong, but excelling at work meant I had a sense of control over some element of my life and my family needed me to earn money and provide a stable and comfortable environment for them. I was caring about the wrong things, one evening after arriving late to the hospital, Lauren unleashed a truthful verbal tirade at me including the hurtful "you care more about work than your own son". "You what, do you know what I am doing for my son and this family? I am killing myself to make sure you all are ok and that I can provide for us, how fucking dare you say that to me" I raged at Lauren, "you haven't even taken paternity leave, that's how much you care" she screamed back at me, before storming off. I was flabbergasted and shocked, how could she say this to me, and why couldn't my mother, sister or Lauren see how hard I was working for my family with all the other plates I had spinning? It was me and my boy against the world, everyone else was clearly against me and ungrateful.

I began believing that no one really cared about me, and I could only rely on my son, I was angry, and I didn't even know why. I was losing my temper and getting agitated over the littlest thing believing the whole world was against me. A siege Mentality that allows me to succeed and flourish at an elite level in my working life but is not conducive to supporting and maintaining long-lasting relationships in my personal. Every conversation with Lauren or family would be a debate or me having to prove I'm right without any room or margin for retrospect, perspective, or empathy, which was not me. If anyone dared to suggest or give advice to me regarding my son, I would absolutely lose my shit and snap back aggressively.

My love and need to protect my son scares me to death, I have to give him everything that I never had. I learned some of life's cruel lessons alone without a father to explain the real world through a man's eyes, prospective and guidance to help navigate and avoid potential life altering dangers and situations. Was it character building for me? Yes, but would I want my son to experience and learn things the way I did? Absolutely not! So, anyone judging my ability as his father or telling me how I should be with him, would quickly be aware in no uncertain terms that their opinion was not welcome, whilst feeling the unforgiving consequences of their poor judgement.

My emotional intelligence radar was completely malfunctioning, I wasn't sympathetic to my tone, facial expression, the way I was saying things or my nonchalant and borderline arrogant body language that I was articulating and gesticulating daily.

I hadn't been working out in the gym, eating healthily, getting enough sleep, or generally looking after myself. I looked and felt a mess, my hands were rough and riddled with eczema from all the washing of hands and anti-bac sanitizer gel used countless times a day. I was accustomed to getting a fresh haircut at my barbers every 10 days or so to keep myself looking well-groomed and professional for work, but it was more than that. Getting a fresh trim would make me feel good about myself and was a form of pampering. My brilliantly skilled barber, Macky, is a perfectionist and would navigate my head and face with attentiveness, skill, and care, I would often fall asleep in the comfortable chair totally relaxed and mentally switched off from rest of the world. The clippers gliding around my head giving a relaxing head massage, the buzzing sound of the razor calming, and the aloe vera hot towel giving me a soothing facial.

I was missing that moment of doing something completely for myself but felt I would be completely selfish to take that time out for me with everything that was happening. It's sometimes the simplest things that are fundamental to a person's mental health and I didn't realise how much I needed my regular haircut for not only the visual impact but more the positive impact on my paternal health. The hair falling off my head and onto my gown was symbolic, like a transformative rebirth, a new me leaving the old me behind that initially entered the barbershop. Luckily, skin to skin with my son was helping to compensate for some of the benefits I was missing out on.

This lack of self-care and poor lifestyle only compounded

the other issues that were plaguing me, and I needed someone to just 'get' what I was going through without me saying it and do something that didn't involve me being quizzed or subjected to any kind of attempted intervention or judgement. It became apparent I was unfairly looking for a clairvoyant or mind reader to just understand what was going on in my frenzied head, which was entirely unjust to my loved ones who had been trying to get through to me with no success, but a nurse called Tracy would make the breakthrough in the most understated and innocuous way.

Our son was making real progress and hitting all the milestones necessary to come home which the doctors said could be within the next week, we first had to show them we could care for him without the assistance of the nurses who had been full time nannies for us, caring for our baby boy 24/7. First up was changing nappies, this was easy, the milky poos weren't so solid, therefore easy to clean up and I had become an expert at changing a nappy in under 21 seconds. Next up was the first bath, this was hilarious, he didn't like it at all and any concerns over his voice or lung strength were quickly removed as I am sure people in the car park could hear his screams and crying as we were attempting to bath him. Whilst holding him aloft like Simba in Lion King, he decided to show us his party trick which involved him weeing and pooing at the same time suspended in mid-air, we were all laughing, the other parents too shared in this beautiful and messy moment, smiling and providing words of encouragement. The final milestone was to come quickly, "are you both ok to stay two nights in one of our private rooms on Thursday and Friday this week?" the doctor asked, "yes we can, that's fine" Lauren responded, this was for them to assess whether we could care for our baby throughout the night with no assistance from any nurses, which is exactly how it would be when we were at home so this was an exciting, nervous, new and welcomed experience for us.

The first night was perfect for Lauren, little man was up every two hours and Lauren was brilliant with getting to him quickly, soothing him by rubbing his back and burping him after his feeds. I couldn't settle, I was sleeping with one eye open, the noises he was making had me on edge and I was suffering from severe anxiety, I kept getting up and checking he was breathing ok.

The nurses gave us good feedback in the morning and surprised us with the news that should "tonight go well again, you will be ok to take your son home tomorrow", Lauren and I looked at each other smiling from ear to ear. I then had to rush off to work, tired but running on adrenaline at the prospect that our beautiful boy could be coming home with us tomorrow. I needed to spend more time with him, around him things were simple, I was calm, relaxed and the frantic pace of my life and mind slowed down to a peaceful evenness when with him.

That evening, I got to the hospital in good time, my market appraisal finished earlier than expected, so Lauren and I had another slap-up meal prepared by head chef Brenda, in the prestigious St Georges Hospital Canteen. With us hopefully going home the next day, it was great to say bye to Brenda who had made the canteen a safe space for me at the candid dad crew during our time there. "Wow, she gave you a big portion", Lauren said, "Yeh, Aunty Brenda always looks after me" I replied. Before leaving, I told Lauren I would catch her up whilst I returned the plates and cutlery. I then pulled Brenda aside, gave her a massive hug and thanked her for treating me like a grandson and I would "continue to eat my vegetables".

Our last overnight stay in the private room was wonderful,

Lauren and I talked about plans for the future, watched our son sleeping and listened to him making the most bizarre but beautiful sounds whilst dreaming away.

In the early hours of the morning, a familiar face popped their head through our room door, "hi guys, I heard you're going home today, so thought I would come in early before my shift to catch you both and say goodbye. Everything will be ok, and you both will be great parents". Tracy had looked after our baby a handful of occasions during his four weeks stay in the neonatal special care unit, but she always made the effort to say hello or pop over to have a quick chat even when she was assigned to different babies. "Thank you so much Tracy for everything you have done for us and our baby" Lauren replied, "Thank you Tracy" I said, voice shaking, tears filling up in my eyes and the biggest lump in my throat that was going to burst like an overinflated balloon.

Her completely selfless and considerate act, supported by words of encouragement not judgement, came from an unconditional loving place. As she left, I quickly fled to the toilet in hallway and cried non-stop for at least 20 minutes, stopping only when someone else knocked on the door to ask how much longer I would be. Tracy's kindness had overwhelmed me, and I was letting out all the stresses, worry, fears, trauma, and emotion that I had been keeping inside since the babymoon in Amsterdam.

The doctor came to see us and gave us the news we had waited weeks for, "you can take your baby boy home", Lauren cried, we were going home and could finally be a real family together, I was elated. But of course, it was never going to be that easy or straightforward. He also said that unfortunately our boy would "need to have an operation for his inguinal hernia, and whilst it was not urgent, it would certainly have to be done within the next few weeks as it was growing." This form of hernia tends to happen when a part of the bowel, such as the intestine, pushes through into the groin at the top of inner thigh.

He already had an umbilical hernia, which is a painless lump near the belly button and is very common in babies born prematurely, the Dr said it could be left as he would most likely grow out of it. I wasn't as fortunate and had to have a hernia op when I was child which gave me an "outie" belly button, but I was near five years old, not 5 weeks old!

I was weary and defeatist. Every bit of positive news we received felt somewhat backhanded to me, underlined with doubt and a 'but' attached to it or with some other worry pending on the horizon. We would be taking him home but knowing we would be back shortly and have to deal with our small premature baby going through the ordeal of a surgical operation under local anaesthetic. I wanted the constant feeling of anxiety to stop, mentally and emotionally I was locking down, I was struggling to come to terms with having, what should be happy milestones and moments, clouded in uncertainty and degrees of peril going from extreme highs to near rock bottom within moments with no control over anything.

"What else is going to happen, for fucks sake" I said, looking up to the heavens, pleading for mercy and a little respite.

In his short time in this world, he had already faced much adversity which was testament to his fight, developing character and strength. Though as new parents, it was the most challenging and scariest time we both had ever faced, I couldn't see the wood through the trees.

Lauren asked, "Are you going to take paternity leave now babe?", we both had agreed that it was wise to not waste those precious two weeks of paternity leave whilst our boy wasn't home yet. As both he and Lauren could benefit more from me being around when we were all at home together, rather than the restricted visiting hours at the hospital and whilst he still had the benefit of the 24/7 care, he was getting from the brilliant nurses in the neonatal special care unit.

I hadn't been a dad for long, but I could already see just how pathetic two weeks paternity leave is for fathers, truly shocking. Never is that enough time to bond with a baby nor provide the stability and support needed to help mothers following childbirth. The financial penalty of taking more time off can often force fathers to go back to work sooner than they would like which is hugely damaging to the family dynamic and can cause irreparable harm to the relationship of father and child due to lack of bond created. This I am sure, could be another contributing factor in some fathers becoming absent, because it is much easier to leave a relationship of any kind if there is a lack of emotional connection and bond with that person. Little did I know that in the coming weeks, I would get all the paternity leave and bonding time with my son I could possibly imagine, due to a virus sharing the same name as a brand of beer!

CHAPTER TWENTY-ONE

~

Placenta

Shortly after given the go ahead to prepare to go home, another doctor we hadn't seen before came into our cubicle to visit Lauren. She was a specialist doctor who was doing a study on Preeclampsia and HELLP Syndrome, to try and understand what causes the conditions, in order to find preventative signs early enough to avoid the high risks of a complicated childbirth. As part of this research, she asked Lauren "if it would be okay for me to study your placenta?", "If it can help other women and stop the severe symptoms I felt and the risk it posed to baby and I, then yes please examine my placenta" Lauren replied, she also offered her services should the doctor require any other information about her experience that could be of help.

The doctor then walked with Lauren to her office to discuss further whilst I got some of our things together in readiness to go home.

The placenta is where the most extensive research on pre-eclampsia is focused. This is due to the organ being responsible for supplying blood from the mother directly to the blood supply of the unborn baby, oxygen and food also pass from mother to baby with waste products from the baby going the opposite direction back into mum. In order to support baby growth, the placenta needs a high volume and consistent supply of blood from the mother, which is the main factor in pre-eclampsia due to the placenta not receiving enough blood which then negatively disrupts the supply between mum and baby. High blood pressure (hypertension) is then caused as a result of elements from the damaged placenta affecting the mother's blood vessels.

They had hooked Lauren up to a machine and placed tabs on her heart and rib, then ran tests to obtain a 360 view of her heart and monitor how well each chamber circulated blood. The findings were that Lauren had a 30 - 40% chance of a heart related issue occurring in her life, and would also be high risk to get preeclampsia in future pregnancies so would need special treatment. Our family would permanently be at the mercy of HELLP, another worry that would linger with us on a daily basis.

There is still no official screening or test that can detect and diagnose with a high level of probability, whether a pregnant woman is at high risk of pre-eclampsia. If every pregnant woman could be screened in the first trimester and then again early in second and third then this could mitigate the unknown for mothers and avoid the emergency complications to childbirth that impacted Lauren so traumatically. Medication and monitoring could then be taken to manage the illness for the safety of mother and child. Ironically, a team headed by leading professor, Basky Thilaganathan, based at St Georges hospital which had been our home for the last 5 weeks, have successfully implemented the UK's first pre-eclampsia screening programme resulting in the decrease of pre-eclampsia by almost 25% as the rate elsewhere continues to rise.

This brilliant team are pioneering this screening process, which clarifies how attentive and comprehensive the hospital was when Lauren first arrived and throughout her journey of giving birth and subsequent aftercare, which now included preventative research by examining Laurens placenta and documenting her experience of preterm pre-eclampsia for further study.

'This study, published by BJOG: An International Journal of Obstetrics and Gynaecology, measured the clinical effectiveness of the Fetal Medicine Foundation (FMF) pre-eclampsia screening programme in a large population of women receiving routine care in a public health setting using retrospective analysis.

The study compared 7720 women who were screened for pre-eclampsia according to the standard NICE risk-based guidance and 4841 by the new FMF algorithm which combines maternal risk factors in the first trimester with blood pressure, a pregnancy hormone, and a Doppler scan measurement. Those at high risk of pre-eclampsia from the FMF algorithm were prescribed 150g of aspirin daily while low risk pregnancies had no aspirin.

The results of the study, which included all singleton pregnancies at St George's between January 2017 and March 2019, showed a 23% reduction in the overall prevalence of pre-eclampsia in the cohort managed with the

FMF screening programme. Over the course of the study, there was also an 80% reduction in women presenting with preterm pre-eclampsia – the more clinically severe form of the disorder.' (https://www.stgeorges.nhs.uk/newsitem/pre-eclampsia-reduced-by-25-at-st-georges-as-rate-increases-elsewhere/)

Professor Basky Thilaganathan, Clinical Director of Fetal Medicine at St George's and Clinical Director of Tommy's National Centre for Maternity Improvement had met with Lauren and I on a number of occasions throughout our time at the hospital and had sat down with us to explain the condition in detail.   In reference to his screening programme, he said: "This screening programme is feasible in an NHS setting and has resulted in a significant reduction of the earliest and most severe form of pre-eclampsia. The continued use of the current maternal risk-factor based preeclampsia screening programme in routine healthcare settings must be re-evaluated".

I had always thought of aspirin simply being a painkiller and had read early on in Laurens pregnancy that aspirin wasn't advised for pregnant women as it may affect the baby's circulation. This only applies to high dose aspirin, low dose aspirin can help prevent heart attack, strokes and lower blood pressure which is one of the main causes of preeclampsia and helps prevent all variations including HELLP syndrome that Lauren had. Generic guidance is that low-dose aspirin should be taken in these instances and the study from St George's FMF team powerfully back this up with the conclusions from their research hard to refute.

If only we had known something so simple and readily available over the counter, could have helped prevent something so severe and life threatening. Lauren would conscientiously take her supplements and folic acid every day without fail, so throwing one low dose aspirin into the mix would have been an easy and much welcomed pill to swallow …

An aspirin a day to keep pre-eclampsia away!

CHAPTER TWENTY-TWO

~

Homecoming

Home. Most people have one but no two are the same, a home is more than a house, way more profound than a structure with a door, windows and pitched roof on top. It's deeper than that. Home for me growing up had a soul and was a sanctuary for me, whatever noise would be going on outside, would be silenced at the front door. Most importantly, home was an emotional connection and an intense sense of belonging, but it wasn't perfect, nothing is. It takes nurturing, protecting and sometimes heart-breaking decisions made that can test a family to the limit, but should toxicity breach the peace that can't be cleansed, then it must be removed for the greater good.

Lauren and I regularly spoke about the environment of our home and how we would raise our son within it, we would disagree on some things but in the main we shared the same ideology and values of what a home would mean for us all. It would be a hybrid of both our upbringings that were vastly different from an ethnic-cultural background, so being able to fuse the best of both thoughtfully, through expression and identification, to ensure our son was exposed and enriched to all his heritage would be pivotal. A home of stability, warmth, love, and respect that represented our values, principles and morals. Mistakes could be made in a safe space, lessons learned, laughs and cries, growth, guidance, and a strong family unit with God in our hearts.

This is the home we would be welcoming our baby into, and it had been a long time coming, but the moment was finally here, the homecoming!

When packing away the last of our things, I flipped through the Redbook again, which I hadn't picked up since it labelled my sons ethnicity as white. I noticed doctor notes regarding the Caesarean birth and the findings literally made my heart stop. I would read that when the doctors delivered him via C section from Laurens's stomach, he entered the world not breathing! He was lifeless! The doctors had to give him assisted breaths using a handheld pump in order to get him breathing, once he caught his breath and his heart started beating again, he was put on the assisted breathing machine and into intensive care! I dropped to my knees in disbelief and in thanks, the shock of these revelations literally took my breath away because no one had told us that this had happened, and it made the fact that we were now taking him home even more special and reminded me of the fragility of life and how quickly it can be taken away.

There were a few practical things I had to take care of before we could leave the hospital with our son, I had to go and collect the baby car seat from home and assemble the buggy to ensure our precious cargo could be transported safely. I was also informed that I had to collect Lauren's milk she had been expressing into the containers that were being stored in the Neonatal unit fridge, I would do this just before we would be leaving.

Whilst Lauren was assisting in research, I was fighting with the car seat to insert it in the backseat of my car, I had asked why we couldn't just have a car seat that doubles up as a baby carrier, but Lauren would not have any of it due to safety issues. She spent extensive time researching the safest baby prams, car seats and cots, to ensure every product was top rated with no compromises being taken with safety.

Lauren came back from her research session with the doctor, "Have you only just finished the buggy, why isn't all our stuff in the car yet?" she said, if only she knew the fight, I had endured with the isofix prongs needed to connect the car seat into place. I looked like I had gone 12 rounds with Mike Tyson, sweating, beaten up and feeling sorry for myself. "Why are you sitting down for? Can you get the milk so we can go home please?" she instructed me, I couldn't even say anything, she had just delivered my king into the world, her favour bag was full to the brim, I had to bite my tongue which I am sure would be a routine I would master.

I had Dave's advice ringing in my ear "don't argue, you can't win those and it's not worth it. Just nod and do what they said with a smile on your face". I nodded, smiled, and said, "no worries my love, I'll get your milk now" and headed to the special care unit. When I arrived, there was not much of her milk in the fridge, so I asked one of the nurses if "this is all of Laurens milk I need to collect?" to which she laughed while shaking her head "oh no no no, there is plenty more of her milk you need to collect. I'll take you to our separate freezer unit" she said, while walking me to a door at the very end of the ward that I had never noticed was there. As we entered, there was a huge chill that slapped me in the face. We were in a walk-in freezer room which was the size of a one-bedroom flat in central London, the nurse then opened another huge fridge which had all of Laurens milk she had been expressing from the time she first produced liquid gold.

I couldn't believe my eyes, Lauren was producing milk at a speed and quantity the unit had never seen before, "She's done so brilliantly well, she could always donate this milk to mothers who can't express milk themselves" the nurse explained. Noble, and definitely something Lauren would happily do to give back, but I had more commercial ideas for her valuable commodity and well-oiled distribution network. I was sure she could start a niche dairy farm, catering to the body building health and cosmetic beauty industry. Markets that so keenly desired the nourishing properties that her milk contained, I had it all planned out and the possibilities were endless with diversification into making in-house organic products forecasted in year 2, expansion into European markets year 3 and worldwide distribution by the end of year 5, fiscal projections that would have Lauren and I multi-millionaires and retired by 40. Maybe Lauren was right after all, I did have talent as a milkman!

I had managed to takeaway two bin liners worth of milk but would have to return to make at least another couple trips such was the vast quantity still needing collecting. As I walked back to the ward from the car park, everything started to slow down for me, the realisation that this would be the last walk I made to the Neonatal special care unit and Lauren, and I were about to take our son home.

Lauren was waiting for me in the kitchen area, we hugged

one another tightly and had a little cry together, this was the moment we had prayed on, hoped on, wished on and manifested to happen and finally it was here. The nurses had him all ready for us, Lauren carefully placed him in the Moses basket and tucked him in tightly with a blanket, and I then carried him out proudly, after we had said our goodbyes to the nurses in the unit who had been phenomenal with not only our new-born son but Lauren. There were a few other nurses we wanted to thank before we left, so we went searching for Dr Polly, Deni, Sophie and Sunita in particular, Tracy we had already said a tearful goodbye too, unfortunately none of them were on shift so Lauren and I vowed to return with our son so we could say thank you and goodbye properly. I have nothing but heartfelt love and thanks for the way those special doctors, nurses, midwives, cleaners, security, chefs, and every other member of staff at St George's hospital, treated and cared for Lauren and my son. I will never be able to repay them for all they did but they will always have our appreciation and support, we are now unofficial and self-acclaimed ambassadors for the hospital.

The walk to the carpark carrying my son was another proud father moment for me, I have never walked more carefully and been more aware of potential hazards and risks in my life. I was stood at a pedestrian crossing until every car had passed and was out of sight, even though cars in both directions had followed protocol and stopped to let us get across. I was taking zero chances. We must have spent twenty-five minutes strapping him into the car seat, worrying that he wasn't secure enough, I understood that worry and anxiety over our son would be with us forever and is something we would have to just live with daily and the responsibility we bear as parents.

Before pulling away out of St Georges Hospital, Lauren

placed her hand on my arm and said, "I can't believe we are parents babe, how do you feel?"

I turned round to look back at my son laying peacefully asleep in the car seat and got vivid flashbacks of my past which had brought me to this moment where I was facing my future, my first child, my son. My heart bursting with love and pride, I inhaled a long deep breath as blissful tears leisurely rolled down my cheeks, and I answered...

"I'm a dad Lauren... I. AM. A. DAD!"

... And I wouldn't change it for anything.

CHAPTER TWENTY-THREE

~

Lockdown Therapy

I never did like the taste of beer!

Taste would be a synonym with continual contextual significance in the coming months, some events palatable and others completely tasteless, literally.

Two weeks after my son came home, Corona virus was rampaging around the world, I wish it was the refreshing summer beer with a sliced lime edged on top going viral. Instead, it was a once in a century Covid-19 virus infecting millions worldwide, a global pandemic with the potential to be as devastating as the 1918 Spanish influenza which infected 500 million people worldwide and killed 50 million.

Within weeks of the first UK case of Covid-19, public guidance from government was to "work from home, where possible" which saw the usually busy roads free from cars and the subscriptions for Netflix tv streaming soar, as people adjusted to their new home-working routine. But as infections began to increase exponentially with our neighbours in Europe who were further on in their Covid journey, the UK officially went into mandatory lockdown, which meant we could only leave our houses if 'absolutely necessary' to get essentials from the supermarket or for time specified daily walks. For many this unprecedented and restrictive policy was like prison and would severely impact peoples mental health, social behaviours, confidence, and emotional stability.

Yet, how could I be locked down to the confines of my house, but yet feel so free and at peace?

In my adult life, I had never taken more than ten days off from work, rarely had sick days, and would always be in holiday allowance deficit at the end of the year, I was the archetypal workaholic. Gold star for me, I was chasing the validation and rewards of what success in my working life brought me, whilst obsessed with being in control of my earnings and the plaudits that come with those professional wins. But that instant hit of dopamine is fleeting and constantly needs to be replaced, as a result I was in a constant state of anxiety to be successful and always ahead of the curve, so petrified of having nothing and being unable to provide for my family living a life of struggle. But this lockdown meant I was being forced to recalibrate and take not just a physical rest but more importantly a mental one, which went against my nature but what my body and mind so desperately needed.

Lauren and I had our Netflix series shows lined up, interrupted only when I had the occasional video catch ups with my sales director to touch base. Whilst the country was

126

locked down, I was having to renegotiate sale prices and ensure the pipeline of sales stayed together and progressed forward, that pipeline was my commission and majority pie of my earnings.

I was doing all the cooking, cleaning, and trips to the supermarket to get provisions, whilst Lauren cared for and fed our baby, this was a new role for me. I was still providing for my family, but doing so in a more holistic and nurturing way and one far more rewarding, with the defining ingredient being the time, not thyme, I was serving up to be available. Though it shouldn't take a global lockdown to be able to provide for my loved ones in this way, as ultimately what was I actually working for? Idealistic sentiment but not realistic, the construct of real everyday life means that in order to provide and maintain a safe space for my loved ones to thrive, means I had to work and create that financial stability with the hope that in time, I could be in a position where I don't have to sacrifice my home life in order to make ends meet. But that happy utopia and balance, takes time... and money!

I was on nappy duty, changing about ten nappies a day, which were on most occasions, toxic milky green explosions which required forensic dexterity to carefully contain and dispose of safely. The green eco bombs were created by mummy, as a result of the nutriments our son was consuming from breastfeeding, he would spend hours suckling and moving from one breast to the other until he passed out milk-drunk, then slept peacefully until he decided to give me more clean-up work to do.

In the beginning I would find it incredibly frustrating when trying to change his nappy because he wouldn't let me, he would close his legs whilst crying. I knew why, he didn't know me, worse yet, didn't trust me. I hadn't earned it, nor should I have been paid it, due to a lack of bonding time between us so we could develop a deeper connection. Coming home with nappies, kissing him on forehead, doing bath and story time before bed was not parenting to form a bond, it was a routine. Being honest with myself, I wasn't doing even doing those things at one hundred per cent, how could I? My working day was taking everything from me and my battery by the time I would come home would need charging. So he and Lauren were barely getting forty per cent of me, I was there in physical form but not the best version that they both deserved. He could sense this, and we both could feel it, love was unconditional of course but the knowing nuance between us was not there, lack of chemistry and rapport, sharing a smile together and that intense look he gave me was like he was saying "oh, you think it's that easy do you? Come on dad".

I was being hard on myself but also truthful, without doubt I was doing the best I possibly could, but this untimely lockdown was going to be my opportunity to connect with my son for a sustained period. Not the pathetic two weeks paternity, leave I didn't even take, which is an impossible period of time for dad and child to form any meaningful bond. Especially when typically, that first four to eight weeks is about mother and baby establishing breastfeeding whilst forming the incredibly important connection that is so pivotal to a babies survival. At that point, dad's role justifiably becomes about being in complete service to mother and child in ensuring both have everything they need, be it food, water, shelter, and all emotional and physical support. However, this period is not dedicated to father getting to bond one-on-one, which is equally as significant, but this imposed lockdown meant I

could be fully invested with no distractions, and I felt
completely liberated by it.

The daily briefings by the prime minister, health secretary
and so-called experts on the death toll, lack of PPE, health
guidance, intensified strain on the NHS, adhering to
lockdown measures and the "following the science" was
becoming ever more depressing. Only the cheering,
clapping, and banging on kitchen utensils in solidarity to the
amazing NHS and public service hero's, gave us all a few
minutes respite of collective joy once a week. In truth,
Covid-19 and lockdown were killing people, just in different
ways.

I found solace in the eyes of my new-born baby boy, he
was oblivious to the chaos that was outside our front door,
nor would he probably believe it when we tried to explain it
to him when he got older. It was like we were in one of
those apocalyptic movies, barricaded inside after dark
hiding away, as that was when the mutant zombies
descended. Whilst adhering to lockdown measures during
daylight which meant rationed essentials at the supermarket
while being two metres apart from other human beings, and
anyone not wearing a mask would be banished and
reprimanded.

On our permitted one hour daily outdoor exercise trips,
we would go for walks with our boy, safely strapped into
my man-harness on my chest. I would then film short vlogs,
which are video blog diaries time stamped, explaining to
him the impact of the pandemic, what was happening that
particular day, conspiracy theories that belonged in
Hollywood scripts, the developmental progress he was
making, and our love for him. So that when he came of age
he could watch it, because it would no doubt appear fairy-

tale, despite this being the reality of what was happening around the world. He would even get to see the crazed apocalyptic zombies, fighting to the death for toilet roll and pasta in the aisles of supermarkets up and down the country. Truly unbelievable, but the truth captured in 4G via Apple iPhone & android, the zombies would be conspiring to put up 5G masts at nightfall!

The bond between my boy and I was going from strength to strength, I would rock him to sleep with one hand as he lay across my forearm, I knew when he needed burping, and he loved when I threw him up and down laughing with the most infectious giggle. Nappy and bath time were our special moments, I would squirt water at him to his delight, he would give me a huge smile with the most amazing twinkle in his eye and I would cream and dress him. It was our personal time to connect, I would talk to him, telling him my dreams for him and how much I loved him. But this was my life, so there would always be something lurking around the corner to test my mental fortitude, nothing was ever simple.

Lauren and I received a phone call from St Georges Hospital, they wanted to perform the inguinal hernia operation on our son, giving us a time and date the following week for it to be done. We were petrified, it was the height of the pandemic, there was a shortage of PPE and people were catching Covid in hospitals when undergoing routine procedures such as the one our son would have.

We couldn't delay it either because the hernia on his groin was the size of a golf ball, he had to have the operation, but there are stable environments in which someone would at least feel comfortable and safe, but this was not it. In fact, this would probably be the worst-case scenario for a preterm baby to undergo an operation under general anesthetic, which would mean he would be totally unconscious and have to stay overnight for observation. I was becoming numb to the feelings of worry, anxiety, stress, and fear, this would be just another stone added to my invisible bag joining some of the other rocks knocking around inside, we all carry these invisible bags, but each bag is different. Throughout our lives we collect various emotional baggage, rocks that enter the bag, and if not emptied they just pile up and become increasingly heavy to carry. These rocks can be heartbreak, depression, stress, guilt, unhappiness, health, work, money, empty battery, identity, rejection, abuse and any other factor or trauma that has happened which goes unresolved, and at some stage the bag needs emptying or the weight of it will pull you down. It's fair to say that my bag was feeling reasonably heavy.

Operation day arrived, we got to the hospital wearing masks and gloves. We had been tested for Covid three days beforehand, using the drive through test centre, I had to put the swab up our son's nose, which was not enjoyable, but we were all given the all clear. The rules said only one parent was allowed in the hospital but since government officials could bend their own rules, so would I, so we got to the operation ward and sat down waiting. They let me stay in the room, while Lauren went with our son and the doctor to the theatre room where they would perform the procedure, I gave him the biggest hug and kiss and repeatedly told him how much daddy loved him. The doctor had said it should take no longer than thirty minutes, to my surprise he returned in twenty confirming it had been successful, Lauren then came back in confirming that she would be staying overnight with him to ensure there were no complications and that she would keep me fully updated.

I picked them up the next morning and thankfully everything was ok, so returned home. The following weeks were a lot calmer, and I was really enjoying the serenity of lockdown, with morning walks through the park, watching my boy evolve and his personality begin to shine through. It was like I was on a retreat to rejuvenate, kangaroo care with my baby was healing me with the positive oxytocin that skin to skin generates, a calming feeling far more sustainable than any instant dopamine hit that success professionally could give me.

Even in a global pandemic and lockdown, work was finding a way to take me away from my family, which meant I couldn't fully switch off, there was always that quick phone call to make, email to make or respond to, or virtual meeting to attend. The consequence of being in the real estate business, money never sleeps, and earnings are completely tied up in commissions and the sentiment of both buyer and seller to conclude the deal that I had so painstakingly worked hard to agree. Within three months the government announced that the property industry would be the first private sector to reopen due to how important the housing market is to the economy, the knock-on impact is immense to retail and in getting the cogs moving on industry in the country.

But I couldn't help feeling that the connection my son and I were making was about to be halted, Lauren was not happy at all, scared for my safety but more so that of our preterm baby, whom I could be putting at risk should I come home and pass Covid to him if picked up during my working day. She was completely right, and I firmly agreed with her, but what could I do? Government guidance which everyone had been following, well majority of us, since the beginning of the pandemic had said I would go back to

132

work. Despite the virus still bring out there killing people and no vaccine yet been found, so the risks were still grave.

I was firmly in-between a rock and a hard place, I wanted to stay at home but many people in the property industry were being furloughed with job security fragile or worst yet, some were being made redundant via conference call. I at least was in a position of having a degree of job security which was not afforded to most and as a leader of people had a responsibility to my team to lead from the front and get business going so they could return to work as quick as possible. Some of them were desperate to return, the harsh realities of lockdown apparent, some were really struggling not having a structure and purpose each day whilst socially being alone was becoming too isolating, negatively impacting mental health.

Family was pulling me to stay at home, but lockdown would never be forever, and love can't put food on the table, financial reasons one of the major divisors of conflict in relationships and central factor in the spiraling rate of divorce. Thus, I saw my time being ripped apart from my family a necessary and pertinent sacrifice for what I believed was the greater good, to work and provide. Contentious topic but I am a man and that is my gender. I respect all who identify as binary, are gender fluid, or have personal pronouns they want to be referred by, but I am profoundly a man, I am he, his and I am him, and one who wants to provide in a traditional sense with core values steeped in respect, whilst embracing an inclusive culture for progressive modern times. Live and let live.

I was battling internal conflict due to government rules, rules being broken in bad taste by said government who set them, which only exasperated the moral dilemma I found

133

myself in by having to leave my family to go back to work, but back to work I did.

It was surreal, the streets were empty, no coffee shops or restaurants open, I was sat in my office with just my assistant manager Daniel, two metres apart, the office had to be rearranged to ensure social distance measures were adhered to. This would be checked by police patrolling every so often, we would go for the odd walk to the parks where masses of people on furlough seemed to be having the time of their lives, Clapham Common had the feel of a festival with boom speakers pumping out hits and a party atmosphere as we stepped over empty cans of flavoured cider.

Though behind the sun kissed faces smiling, there was an eerie feeling of jeopardy in the eyes of many, their futures uncertain and many of them were in fact already unemployed but just didn't know it yet. Furlough was just a stay of execution, a long kiss goodnight, which was utterly sobering, I would go back home counting my blessings because the harsh realities of the world quickly remind you that romantic idealism can't stop the juggernaut train of economic capitalism. Come the end of the month the bills would be swiftly collected from my bank account by courtesy of direct debit, leaving a bitter taste in the mouth, a symptom also accompanying Covid.

CHAPTER TWENTY- FOUR

~

Bubble Love

My mother hadn't held her grandson for months now, out of fear that she could pass coronavirus onto him, or we pass it her, as she was in the 'vulnerable' category due to her age. I would make regular trips most days so she could see him through the window, or I would hold him up aloft in the air like Rafiki did Simba in the lion king, which would draw the happiest smile from her. This was typical of my mother, always trying to do the right thing even when it is at the detriment of herself. I would continually try and make her hold my son and kiss him, but she wouldn't have any of it, I would say "mum, no one is going to know, its fine", she would firmly say 'no', reiterating that it was against the rules, a risk to everyone's safety and reminding me about the importance of having integrity "doing the right thing, even when no one is watching you". I had heard this sermon frequently when growing up, and of course she was, as always, correct! She was again setting the standard and expectations of what is right and wrong and how to behave, but this was my opportunity to be in complete service to her as she had always been to my sister and I. Making sure she was ok every day, doing supermarket runs so she had food and other essentials to be comfortable, and having some mother and son in-person chats that we both would desperately need for our mental health, even if I was stood outside the front door and her sat at the bottom of the stairs inside.

"Be grateful and pray for small mercies, through the grace of god" she would say, to be thankful for what we have, as the little things are usually the most important. I understood this now more than ever, growing up as a child the world was a small place with school, home and church on a Sunday being the weekly routine. I would want to stay in on a Sunday morning watching cartoons, but I would be made to polish my shoes and put on my 'Sunday best clothes' to attend church to give thanks at 10am mass. Once there I would always feel at peace and leave happy I went, hymns being sung, bible passages read, the organ being played with choir in sync and religious stories heard that would apply to what was happening in the world at that time. The wonder of Jesus turning water into wine, divine, but I saw my mum perform greater miracles!

Growing up, the cost of living and recessionary tales of hardship weren't just consequences of macro global events, this was a daily occurrence of sacrifice, mercy, and love, that I witnessed my mum performing in my household.

Sunday dinner, we would have all the trimmings, but that meal would last through to at least Tuesday that week. Leftovers the following day, she would then transform the chicken carcass into a delicious soup, sometimes she wouldn't eat or would wait to see what my sister and I left on our plates, we wasted nothing! She knew how to make money stretch and get the most value out of every penny spent, Supermarkets were fleeting occurrences, Saturday mornings we would head to the market to buy fish, meat, and our humble weekly needs, not wants. I would be dragged along up and down the market whilst my mum haggled with fruit and veg stall vendors to negotiate the best possible price in order to get the most out of her pound coin. "The vendor down the end there is charging ten pence cheaper" she would confirm, you see, she had done her market research so to speak, unbeknown to me but this vibrant trading setting would be the perfect marketplace where I would get lessons in salesmanship, value, price, negotiation, inflation, supply, demand, and soft skills. These were business teachings, so many people know the cost of everything but the value of nothing, I did. I never enjoyed carrying the heavy bags of produce home though, but I had to contribute and work for my dinner. I used to watch her dilute the heavily concentrated washing up liquid with water which would prolong its usage as, "a little goes a long way", she often said, these type of life hacks would subconsciously stay with me, engrained in my psyche and form my habitual actions later on in life.

I never had free school dinners, the choice for her to work full time rather than make fiscal gains from claiming benefits, meant that she/we were disadvantaged, so I had homemade packed lunches every day. She would fill up an empty bottle of water with blackcurrant squash, and I had to bring that same bottle back home so it could be refilled the next day. My sandwiches were perfectly formed, I liked them cut halves not diagonal, cheese and pickle were my filling of choice but would be on a rota. This is where my business acumen and entrepreneurship spirit would grow, I would sell the sandwiches most days for £1, sometimes more, depending on how weighted the supply and demand scale was tilted in my favour, chicken and chips after school was on me should an open auction have occurred where my returns were in excess of 400%. I would then reinvest 20% of my profits and buy an 8 pack of doughnuts for 80p and then sell them individually to my school friends for 50p each, a profitable enterprise for me with seismic profit margins. I would never forget however, that it was my mums initial sandwich making investment that facilitated my thriving sole trader business, my Saturday morning education trips to the market with my mum were already paying out handsome dividends.

My school shirts were always crisp white, my mum would soak them overnight in the bath, then be on her knees hand scrubbing the cuffs, arm pits and collar areas which caused her hands to have calluses. You see, no child of hers would be going to school with dirty collars and people would always comment on how well presented we were which would often fill her with pride, something she instilled in my sister and I. As we got older we needed our own space, Lisa being five years older, I was the annoying little brother invading her teenage privacy. My mum decided to move to our smaller shared bedroom and partitioned her larger room into two, so we could both have our independence and room.

Holidays abroad were few and far between but when we did go away, it was to see family in Jamaica or New York which were unappreciated at the time, but wonderful experiences for us to have had as children, especially considering the expense of visiting these long-distance premier destinations on one sole income. Margate, Brighton and other seaside trips were a big part of our upbringing with mum trying to expose us to as much as possible to broaden our horizons and see sights that weren't seen on our day-to-day shores of southeast London.

I have no regrets about the things I didn't have or may have missed out on, only profound admiration, respect, and love for what my mum did for me. When your young you think some of your friends have more than what you do based on materialism and what is cool in school, when in fact I had everything I needed to set me up in life and I was fortunate enough to receive these material gifts each and every day. Examples of love, sacrifice, worth ethic and trying to do the right things, saving, and prioritizing for what is truly important. I would watch her sit in the dining room with the door closed writing dissertations by hand to further better herself, witness her get numerous promotions at work where she was a leader of people and ran departments. I attended her university graduation ceremony just as she had clapped proudly up in the rafters whilst my sister and I graduated through the education system to university level - another example of her practicing what she preached. I witnessed her buy the property we lived in to set the example that working hard, having ambition, and saving money means you can "have a piece of something in this world, that you own". All of these feats and so much more I witnessed her accomplish, and do so with no helping hand, all by HERSELF! These were the real soulful anecdotes of my childhood that I encountered, which didn't have the clout or bragging power at school that the latest PlayStation console or Nike air max 95 trainers would receive but would give me the sustainable footing and supportive insoles to walk my personal path and flourish, stood firmly and confidently on my own two feet.

To this day, sadness occurs when she recalls the experience of being out shopping with Lisa as a child and she asked my mum for an ice cream as they passed an ice cream van, but at that time in life she couldn't afford it and had to tell my sister 'No'. Mum will still shed a tear when recalling that traumatic moment, which is a reminder of how money can influence happiness but also how not having it can cause immense hardship that can, if the pain is harnessed positively, fuel a relentless drive to better your life and those around you. I know that chilly ice cream moment will in some part form how she will be with my son, most likely bubble wrap him with love and shower him with treats as most grandparents do, to overcompensate for some of the things she may feel we missed out on or had to be sacrificed for the greater good. The relationship she has with my son will be special and one that will allow me to get a small glimpse of how she was with me which I will find enlightening to see in real time, capturing and appreciating every second, as life is precious.

Thankfully the government introduced a different kind of, but enormously welcomed, bubble of support. One that meant my mum could finally wrap her loving warmth around my son, because this lockdown bubble could be formed by linking two households together as restriction measures were relaxed a little, so my mum could get to start forging that special bond with her grandson that she had missed out on. This made lockdown a lot easier for Lauren and I, knowing that my mum was helping our little family and we too were equally helping her from loneliness which was equally contagious as coronavirus, due to lockdown isolation.

Meanwhile, I was at work navigating a new world of distancing socially from other human beings, wearing masks and gloves every day in the height of summer, with my hands brutally sore from the aggressive use of anti-bac hand sanitizer. Whilst operating in a state of complete fear desperately trying not to get Covid, because there was still no vaccine approved for roll out and I was the primary threat to my loved ones of bursting the bubble of love we had created.

CHAPTER TWENTY-FIVE

~

Renovation To Restoration

23rd March 2020, a date that would be forever etched in our minds, the day the UK went into a full mandatory lockdown. I had miraculously managed to get my flat sale through to exchange, and house purchase completed just one week before we were restricted to our homes and just in time for Lauren and I to bring our son home from hospital.

This was a massive relief and weight off my shoulders as the pressure to get both over the line was getting more intense and thankfully a few of those heavy rocks in my invisible burden bag had been removed. In preparation of doing some major works to the property, I had detailed architect plans drawn up for a loft conversion and kitchen extension, to afford more living and entertaining space downstairs, whilst doubling the number of bedrooms upstairs to cater for guests and futureproofing any potential additions to our family. However, the uncertainty of Covid meant I had tough decisions to make about whether to go ahead with the renovation works or not, with a host of considerations to contemplate. Should I be putting my seven-week premature new-born baby through building works? The house was perfectly liveable, and works could be delayed, my job was heavily commission based and with lockdown and uncertainty of furlough, was it prudent to spend my life savings at a time where no revenue was coming in due to the economy being completely shut down? These were just some of the dilemmas I had to work through, but in the end Lauren firmly pushed for more living space and making the kitchen the heart of our home, so we decided to do the kitchen rear extension whilst pausing the loft conversion until a later date.

I clearly am a glutton for punishment, majority of people who had just been through all I had would be forgiven for wanting a prolonged period of harmony and tranquillity, not me, within weeks of our decision to press ahead with major renovations, the builders were knocking on the door at 6am to begin. It was the 18th May, I was starting to feel that pacy on-edge feeling of anxiety again, realising that I had just added more hefty rocks to my bag than the few I had recently discarded, the emotional baggage was now feeling heavier than before. It dawned on me that I was back at work before any other private sector industry putting my health at risk, pumping my life savings into building works, uncertainty over my income due to global pandemic, and the realisation that my son had only been home for eight weeks so the opportunity and time I thought I had to bond with him had gone in a blink of an eye.

I was now to embark on a testing period of time because within a week of works being underway, Lauren declared that she was going to stay with her mum and taking our son, due to the dust now taking over the house. It was probably the right decision, but it felt like a dagger to the heart, Lauren leaving me to deal with the uncomfortable situation alone taking my son too, where was my support coming from? Are relationships not supposed to be ride or die through thick and thin? through hardship and adversity? It felt like she was running away at the first speck of dust to leave me to manage it all, she then would come back once all the hard graft had been done to then enjoy the fruits of my labour. I wasn't happy at all, but it was in our baby boy's best interest to be in a safe and clean environment, it just meant my days got longer and I was doing more running around from the building site, to work, to Laurens mum place and then back again. I didn't want to leave the house empty and exposed for security reasons, which meant I would often get back to the house late at night after seeing my boy and Lauren after work.

In truth I didn't like staying at her mums, I was a grown man who had been living alone for over a decade, so it was hard having to dance to someone else's tune and feel like I had to tip-toe around being respectful when I just wanted to hold my son skin to skin and spend quality time with, he and Lauren. As the weeks and months progressed, I would find my house a safe haven to retreat to and have some alone time for a few hours, but the conditions were grim.

The downstairs of the house was a no-go area, there was no hot water or heating, and I was living out of one room with a microwave, bottled water and a hope that the works would finish ASAP, the cold showers were not enjoyable. The way the main builder would call me last minute at the end of the week for "money to pay my guys", you would think I had a money tree to shake, I was parting with tens of thousands of pounds most weeks and yet still months away from completion. That wasn't the only expensive toll I was paying, my job was also taking a strain on me due to the level of commitment, drive and time required to run a successful real estate office. It's not an archetypal 9 to 5 job where you can switch off at the end of the day, you take the job home with you, work overtime, weekends and it consumes a massive part of your life, which can compromise other things at the expense of, even if it is for, others.

Our son was developing well with his character growing together with his weight, one night we would get a first glimpse of him trying to push boundaries to establish what power and influence he had. Lauren was trying to put him to sleep, doing the usual feed before bed, but it was taking unusually longer than normal. After an hour she called me upstairs because he was crying uncontrollable, I had developed a rapport with him which meant he settled easier with me. This involved me singing classic hit songs, most notably by Boys II Men, Whitney Houston, and Michael Jackson, those would be the artists he settled and dozed off to quickly but, on this occasion, my vocal prowess was doing nothing but to antagonise and irritate him further.

We tried burping him, rocking him, feeding him, walking around with him but nothing worked, and his banshee-like screams caused Lauren's mum and sister to rush into the bedroom concerned, such was his apparent distress. The only option was to take him to the hospital, fortunately St George's hospital was a short trip away, so we got him ready. I had come straight from work so all I had was some old jogger bottoms shrunk two sizes too small, white socks and a t shirt, I would have to complete this shabby-chic look with my formal work shoes and overcoat. I said to Lauren and her family, "I think he is ok; this is a test to see what he can get away with" but rightfully they weren't going to take the risk, nor was I! So I carried him downstairs and put him in the car seat, at this stage the cries and pitch of the sobs were getting ever softer.

By the time we got to the hospital he was quiet, but we were here now so may as well get him checked out. As the car park flood lights shone upon me, I couldn't help chuckle at what my son had me leaving the house looking like. I certainly wouldn't be winning any GQ magazine awards for best dressed male, instead I was committing heinous, visual crimes to humanity. Fashion faux pas indeed, but I had to own it, I'd learnt that you do anything with enough confidence and swagger then people assume it must be on purpose. So here I was, rocking my Gucci loafers, white socks, ripped t-shirt, joggers that were more like shorts and overcoat draped over me, whilst holding my son like a new season Louis Vuitton bag. I strutted through that emergency room pouting and focused, head held high and shoulders back, like I was walking for Tom Ford at New York fashion week. The looks from patients were of complete bewilderment and sickness, but it was clearly because they were not on-trend.

As suspected, shortly after arriving at the hospital, our son was fast asleep in his buggy. This was all part of his masterful plan, he was testing me, at best testing boundaries but at worst it was a power move to establish his influence and control, asserting his stanch will over us. If this was business, he was attempting an aggressive takeover, a coo, he wanted my corner office and to show what kind of circus he could fashion, by having us running around performing elaborate tricks after him, belonging to a cirque du soleil show. To be fair to him, I was definitely dressed the part of a clown.

We were seen to very quickly and the nurse did some routine checks and confirmed everything was ok and we could go home, I still had to go back through the hospital doing the catwalk of shame and was too tired to pout. The looks this time were of pity fused with the odd smile of empathy and compassion, I'm sure this would be the first of many similar situations at the behest of my son. It was obvious he would keep us on our toes, and I would need to have a constant eye on him, I had already been sleeping with one eye open, keeping a woke gaze on him, developing massive nervousness in me. A consequence owing to his issues when born, he came into this world not breathing and needing a hand pump to draw his first breath, then a machine to assist him, and the erratic noises he would make when asleep meant I was in panic mode if I couldn't hear or see him. I knew this feeling of worry would always be there as a parent and accepted I would just have to live with it.

It was the beginning of December and the country had recently gone back into another national lockdown. The finish line with the house renovations was in sight, a three-to-four-month project had overrun by more than the same initial timescale. At this point, 2nd December 2020, the Pfizer-BioNTech Covid-19 vaccine was approved for us in the UK, becoming the first to be authorised anywhere in the world. Finally, a vaccine that would pave the way for a sustainable roadmap for normality to return in the near future, which would help kickstart growth in the economy, other industries would then slowly be coming back off-furlough, and everyone could readjust to the lost year of lockdown.

"This needs to be finished by Christmas" I had barked at the builders, my patience waning and frustration bubbling to boiling point as we were getting painfully close to the 25th December and seven months into a project supposed to take just three. They managed to meet that hard deadline, which was relieving, though they really took it to the wire. It was Christmas Eve, but the house still wasn't ready for us to move into yet, it needed a thorough clean and much of our belongings would need to be moved back in.

Yet I stood in the new kitchen space observing the completion of a vision and all the sacrifices it took to get here whilst having inventive ideas about furniture placement and soft furnishings. Lauren would surprisingly interrupt my creative process, "They took too long, and there's still snagging, I'm not moving in yet" she said, I understood what she was saying but couldn't we just take a grateful moment to look at the amazing contemporary space created and the painstaking refurbishment of the entire house? Our sons beautiful new bedroom, the Parisian inspired panelling throughout complimenting the early nineteenth century Victorian fabric of house. The refined and deep chalky pigmentation of farrow & ball paint adorning the walls, a costly coat, the high skirting boards, and grey tone parquet flooring. The two-metre-wide lantern dome facilitating natural light to stream into the kitchen during the day and to stargaze at night, the floor to ceiling bi-fold doors to create indoor-outdoor living, and the large centrepiece - a waterfall marble stone island and polished concrete floor with matt black kitchen units. I even got the instant hot water/sparking Quooker tap, paying homage to the market appraisal I conducted on the day I found out Lauren was pregnant. Elderflower cordial already on the shopping list!

There was so much to feel proud of and happy about in that moment, especially given this was all done in a global pandemic with all the challenges that caused. So I was left feeling a little disappointed that Lauren was focusing on there being no stopper behind the door, or that one of the shelves wasn't completely flush. Majoring in the minors, as opposed to looking at the Pinterest worthy home that had been created, with me effectively project managing and interior designing the entire renovation by myself.

A simple "well done Paul, thank you" would have sufficed, I mean, it was largely for her and our son, and this was the outcome of the sacrifice and hardship over these turbulent pandemic lockdown months and before. In this instance I needed a cheerleader, there would be time for snagging and meticulous dissecting of finishing, but this was not the time. "Please don't critique when I'm dreaming and creating" I said, just once I wanted to savour this big win and enjoy the present in real time.

I stood underneath the lantern looking up at the stars, reminiscing back to the last time I looked up at the night-time sky, that Starry Night at the hospital almost a year ago to the day. So much had happened and changed, I was pondering about the past but looking ahead to what the future held for my family and what this new world post pandemic would look and feel like.

There would be the question that would divide and curate relentless debate; "Have you been vaccinated?" creating as big a divide as Brexit did, while people's belief system and rights for privacy and choice was challenged and defended. Restoration, a period of heeling and calm is what I craved most but with the niggling sensitivity that there was still structural issues that needed to be resolved. The works may have been finishing on the house but it felt like remedial underpinning on the foundations of our relationship were only just beginning with Lauren I. Adapting to our new family dynamic and how being a mother would impact her own identity, I had already begun seeing the subtle seeds of resentment budding, feeling like I was getting the culpability for the fact women get pregnant and men don't or that I was still having the privilege of going to work each day which she somehow deemed akin to me vacating on some exotic luxury day trip away.

When I left the house each morning at 7am, with my double-breasted suit of armour, gloves, and mask on. It definitely wasn't a holiday camp I was heading towards; many a boot would continuously be kicking my behind throughout the course of the battling working day. Leaving me not a very happy camper by the time I came back home in the evening.

Despite my frustration I understood I had it easy, acknowledging how difficult it would be for Lauren and not just her, all women. Their careers, earnings, social status, and personality goes under modification when becoming mothers, their lives literally changing overnight. I could see Lauren already starting to feel like she was losing elements of who she was. Friends stopped calling her to go out, the routine of putting makeup on and getting dressed for work halted, career paused, and her body changed from the model figure she was happily accustomed to seeing in the mirror. The impact on self-identity and self-worth is an eventuality of motherhood and whilst I couldn't relate physically, I definitely empathised emotionally. I would endeavour to absorb any vented anger when I got home a few minutes later than expected, missing bin collection day or forgetting to load the dishwasher. These small little things that would seem somewhat inconsequential to me after a manic day at work, would be the big things that made her feel like I didn't care or that she was taken for granted. Those small things would have to be big things to me too, quickly moving up on my priority list as we transitioned into a new stage of not only our lives but our relationship.

Lauren was going through a transformational period, and I would have to transform with her and both of us communicate better. Communicating with understanding and empathy, whilst being sympathetic to tone and pitch, as we were both strong characters and inherently stubborn. Most importantly we would need to listen to the other persons views and perspective so we could be on the same page, a team!

CHAPTER TWENTY-SIX

~

Two Syllables, One Word

Christmas Day was at my mum's house, and we all enjoyed a great day. After dinner the music was playing loud as my mum poured me a big glass of ice-cold sorrel. It was exactly 12 months ago I was getting a similar glass poured but I was at the hospital ward back then. I got goosebumps, my son then reached out to me, having had enough of his Aunty Lisa dancing with him around the kitchen. I sat him on my lap, my face resting on the back of his head, Whitney Houston then came through the speakers, the greatest love of all song.

I don't know what was coming over me but the lyrics were doing something to me, moving me, "Everybody searching for a hero, People need someone to look up to, I never found anyone who fulfil my needs, A lonely place to be, And so I learned to depend on me, I decided long ago, Never to walk in anyone's shadows, If I fail, if I succeed, At least I'll live as I believe, No matter what they take from me,

They can't take away my dignity". That verse spoke to me loudly and resonated deeply as memoirs from my journey. The first verse was like a scripture to follow, values and teachings in order to get the best out of my son and my obligation to him as his dad; "I believe the children are our future, teach them well and let them lead the way, Show them all the beauty they possess inside, give them a sense of pride to make it easier, Let the children's laughter remind us how we used to be".

By the time the song had got to the chorus again, I had to leave the room, son in my arms I rocked him in the hallway as the song reached the crescendo, "Because the greatest love of all, is happening to me, I found the greatest love of all, inside of me, the greatest love of all, Is easy to achieve, Learning to love yourself, It is the greatest love of all". Tears were flooding from my eyes, they wouldn't stop. It was if I was going through a spiritual rebirth or awakening, a baptism of sorts. My son was evidently my mecca whom I worshipped, so it felt essential to go through this rite of passage, a ritual to crush and obliterate the rocks from my unseen baggage bag.

Every teardrop falling from my eyes were a burden healed away, I was left feeling lighter, calm, happy and with renewed optimism about what the next year and beyond would be like. It would be my son's birthday the next day where he would be one years old, his birthday presents under the same Christmas Tree waiting to be opened but he would surprise me with, the greatest love of all, so to speak to see in the New Year.

Our son had turned one years old on Boxing Day, a seminal moment for Lauren and me. I convinced myself that he needed the Yamaha piano I got him, but it was really a gift for me, much like that Dyson fan I got 'for him'. Growing up I had always wanted to play that instrument, it was something about the sound of the keys, melodic. Probably influenced by the soulful music I had heard growing up in my household as a child, it was just another layer for the environment of serenity and melodic peace I was so desperate to create. I sat him on the Piano, adjusting the seat high enough so he could reach, and his first attack of the keys was as if he had played before. The totally random pressing of notes was chaotic harmony, he clearly had a natural gift for major and minor scales which immediately struck a chord. It filled me with joy, one tick beside a column from the missing wants of my childhood. My son had already got something I had so wished for, I would remind him often how lucky and privileged he was to have the gift of a musical instrument in his home, he soon composed his appreciation to me through another form of cord that would hit a pitch and note sonically, that he would struggle to ever better its impact on me.

New Year's Eve was a few days away, and I was already getting mentally prepared to return to work the following week. I had also started writing my goals which I did before every new year, this involved manifesting personal and professional objectives to elevate and grow me as a person.

I had just got home from the supermarket, and as soon as I walked through the door, Lauren screamed excitedly, "Paul, he said his first words, dada". I dropped the shopping down and ran over to him, almost tripping over the stairgate, "say it again son" I said. He looked at me wide eyed and smiling for about 10 seconds, then his mouth moved creating the most perfect two-syllable vocal symphony that I had ever heard, "dada". Cue euphoria!

His first words, "dada", this was validation, approval, a choice he made. I felt special, proud, deeply grateful and thankful. It was at this moment I truly felt like a dad, he claimed me and honoured me. Doing so with words, words I had so often struggled with vocalising in my life, speech, free but didn't speak out so freely to me. It's like he would be all the positives to my negatives, completing me and he would become a better version of me, he knew I needed to hear "dada", not just for that instance but for its power on the rest of my life.

I had always sensed this special spiritual connection with him from the first instance we laid together skin to skin, he was my soul, and mate, as well as my son. Like most boys he will undoubtedly be a mummy's boy, just like I was, but I would always have this special moment of his first words being for me and to me. No bonus, reward, award, promotion, commission, or thrill of closing a deal would ever come close to this feeling, HELLP couldn't stop me, and help wasn't needed, my son had just let me know that I was doing a good job and I was more than just a father to him. I was his "dada", his dad.

Every hardship suffered in my life up to this point felt like it was worth it and supposed to happen precisely this way on purpose, so that I could experience this supernova sensation. Whilst poignantly reflecting upon the realisation that there is no weakness to be found in the strength of answering the calling of becoming a dad, and to give a child the belief and freedom to imagine, dream, and soar to the stars without fear…

That's the love of dad.

The End.

HELLP! I'M GOING TO BE A DAD!

ACKNOWLEDGEMENTS

~

To say that I could never have envisioned writing a book is more than an understatement but having gone through this cathartic exploration of self-reflection and discovery, it became apparent that I was truly destined to. Constantly having so much to say but my stammer often suppressing my speech, it only makes sense for my words to be heard visibly through the retina of a reader's eyes.

Concluding this book took a lot longer than expected but it wasn't a choice it was a calling, and each time I was sure it was finished, I found I had something more to say. It became an essential means of therapy for me, confronting deep-rooted trauma, insecurities, and truth. Revisiting my past, to face to my future.

Born out of a lived experience, this book is an emotive expression of realism immersed in non-fiction, therefore the people I am acknowledging have been influential to not just the pages of this book but the sacred scriptures of my life. Some of you I've known forever and others less than a lifetime, but you all deserve these flowers of gratitude in what is one of the proudest achievements that I will most likely ever accomplish.

There is only one person I can begin with to thank first. To Lauren, eternal love, and thanks for protecting, loving, and bringing our perfect son into the world. What we went through together this book tells only half the story told through my lens, but the strength and sacrifice you showed through the entire pregnancy and childbirth journey there are simply no superlatives or words, that can do you justice. This book is a testament to your experience too and therefore a timeless gift of acknowledgement. Your life-threatening ordeal with Pre-Eclampsia and HELLP syndrome was astonishing, but your spirit extraordinary, and you survived. Saving both yourself and our son, who can be forever proud and blessed that he has a fighter and superhero for a mother x

To my son, Hunter Maverick Bent, this book is dedicated to you and wouldn't exist without you. I hope to set positive examples and be a man you can admire, respect and be proud to call 'dad'. I will make many mistakes but will keep trying to do the right thing and you won't sometimes understand the decisions I have made but just know that I'll always have your best interests at heart. Always remember our core values that we say each morning together and try to live by; To be kind, to be fair, and have respect. Everything I do is with you at the centre of it and when you are old enough to read and understand this book, you'll get to know more about who daddy is, in a deeper and more meaningful way. My past experiences, my feelings, and my life up to this point, in my own words. This is my legacy to you H, I love you son x

I would like to give huge thanks to all the wonderful staff at St Georges Hospital for the exceptional care they provided to Lauren and our preterm baby boy, their warmth, dedication, and specialist expertise I could never fully repay but hopefully this book goes a small way in showing my gratitude and wholehearted thanks.

To my family located around the world, I feel your warmth in every text message, phone call or personal embrace we share. To Uncle Earl, Aunty Gloria, Aunty Cynthia, Aunty Pauline, Uncle Colin, Cousins; Camille, Rochelle, Heather, Richard, Conroy and Dwayne, I love you. To Marlene & Bertie, huge thanks for everything you have done for us. For being more than just friends, but extended family members, not by blood, but pure heart and devotion.

Now, to the two most influential people in my life. The love, admiration, and appreciation I have for you both is adorned throughout the pages of this book, but official acknowledgements couldn't be written without me dedicating a few more sentences to the incredible women who helped shape and raise me.

To my sister Lisa, your continuous support, guidance, and advice, that I mostly never listen to, is always welcomed, and treasured. Thank you for always being my biggest fan, setting positive examples, and for trailblazing five years ahead of time so that my road has clearer signs, and the 'right' turns forward. Massive love for also never telling mum about the secret house parties I had when she was away in Jamaica, love you sis.

My unbelievable mother, I can't thank you enough for what you have done for me, and I couldn't love you anymore than I do. You are the driving force in my life and everything good in me is because of the example set by you, I am the embodiment of the sacrifices, hard work and aspirations you endured and had for me. I know I gave you some tough times, but I hope you are proud of the man I have become and feel like I have more than made up for those bad school reports. You always say that you've never seen me "pick up a book and read", so thought I would write one instead!

To all my friends, thank you for our conversations, the many lessons you haven't realised you taught me and the experiences we have shared together. In particular, two of my oldest friends Eward Richards and Paul Francis for a lifetime of brotherhood, and while we may not speak every day or see each other as often as we should, your contribution to my life and to this book as fellow dads can't go unwritten.

Special acknowledgment to Daniel Montaque, whom I have enjoyed seventeen, and counting, years of friendship that I never take for granted, you have observed my evolution and been a rock beside me throughout much of my journey. We have walked similar paths in our lives with our suits cut from the same cloth, a dynamic duo custommade with intricate seams of support, hemmed with perspective and embroidered in motivation that has been immeasurably valuable to me, tailored immaculately in truth and dressed in love. I hope I've provided you with an equally fitting service of friendship as you have to me, thank you bro!

Hej JK, thank you for the emotional support and harmony you provided me through the challenging latter stages of writing this book. In the vulnerable stillness of silence deep truth is revealed, and you helped me block out the noise by being a safe place of escapism and mindfulness without judgement. You have a special gift of being able to be completely present and to listen, which is a selfless act of generosity I really appreciate in you and value enormously, Tak.

Huge acknowledgement to all my work colleagues past and present, with special recognition to the KFH family. You provided me with an opportunity as a young boy to attack adulthood at a pace way beyond my years, raising my expectations, maturity, access to growth and embodied a culture of values overlapping the ones I was raised by, a heartfelt thank you.

I would like to thank my brilliant illustrator Ana Latese, for bringing my artistic vision to vibrant life, your talented strokes capturing the subtle gestures between my son and I, whilst beautifully evoking the spirit and sentiment of the book.

Many of my childhood inspirations are featured in chapter one, however there were fictional characters portrayed on screen that influenced me just as profoundly from a role model perspective. Thank you, Eddie Murphy for Marcus Graham in Boomerang and for Hakeem in Coming to America. Thanks to Will Smith for Fresh Prince of Belair, and for Mike Lowry in Bad Boys! These characters were part of my household growing up, I wanted to be like them, I even used to wear my school blazer inside out copying Will in Fresh Prince, and they evolved with me over the years. From VHS tape to DVD and now online streaming, these characters acted out authentic parts in my characteristics. An impactful series of role plays still filming through me to this day, a nostalgic and real manifestation of life imitating art.

Flowers of appreciation to all the women and mothers who are survivors of Pre-eclampsia & HELLP syndrome. Sincere thanks to both APEC, 'action on pre-eclampsia', and St George's Hospital that are doing life changing, and saving, research to help prevent and detect this condition.

Thanks to all the dads and men who will read this book and hopefully feel empowered to talk and express ourselves, to be seen and be heard. We don't have to keep things inside to live up to false narratives, stereotypes, or toxic expectations. Let's discard some of these heavy rocks we carry and keep hidden away in silence that weigh us down and promote conversation and action around paternal health. We have a fundamental part to play and are absolutely essential in the pregnancy process, as birthing partners and most importantly, as dads. I hope my story helps inspire others to tell theirs.

To end, I would like to thank the person who was always brave enough to go against the grain, believe in themselves and have an opinion. The individual who didn't let perceived weaknesses stop them from expressing themselves and having a voice. That always smiled, was respectful and well-mannered with a quiet confidence and determination. Who never let their shine be dimmed or allowed others to minus their pluses, believing in their principles and values with God in their heart.

I would like to thank that young Black British-Caribbean boy from Lewisham, South East London, that was ambitious and wanted to get the maximum out of his potential. But could have easily made many of the wrong choices, preventing the right positive outcomes, but for whom I'm forever grateful to, proud of and love.

This stupendous and magnificent person, who deserves this special recognition unreservedly is…

Me.

ABOUT THE AUTHOR

~

Paul Bent is a real estate expert and inspirational speaker, using his voice to build safe spaces through his work with young people, to help inspire future generations and be a role model to those without one. Sharing his lived experiences, Paul intends to passionately promote positive narratives of fatherhood through his writing, striving to give new fathers an authentic and impactful insight into the extraordinary excursion of parenthood.

Witnessing first-hand the impact of Pre-eclampsia and HELLP syndrome on mothers and the whole family. He aims to raise more awareness of this illness, and to give women a rare look into a man's psyche to endorse communication and understanding, vividly told through his words.
Paul is a loving dad to a son and lives in London.

Follow him socially on Twitter/Instagram: @pb_speech or scan him below.

PB_SPEECH

BIBLIOGRAPHY

~

Preeclampsia Foundation 2021, *preeclampsia organisation website*, accessed 10th January 2022, <https://www.preeclampsia.org/hellp-syndrome>

NHS 2021, *NHS website*, accessed 21st December 2021, <https://www.nhs.uk/conditions/pre-eclampsia/>

Healthline Media 2022, *Medical news today website*, accessed 21st April 2022. <https://www.medicalnewstoday.com/articles/252025#causes>

NCT 2018, *NCT organisation website,* accessed 22nd March 2022, <https://www.nct.org.uk/pregnancy/worries-and-discomforts/pregnancy-related-conditions/hellp-syndrome>

Olivia Wohlner, 2020, *New beauty website*, Accessed 7th June 2021, <https://www.newbeauty.com/what-is-colostrum/>

Mayo foundation for medical education and research 2023, *Mayo Clinic Organisation website,* Accessed 12th July 2021, <https://www.mayoclinic.org/diseases-conditions/premature-birth/diagnosis-treatment/drc-20376736>

The Nemours Foundation 2021, *Kids health organisation website*, Accessed 12th November 2021. <https://kidshealth.org/en/parents/preemies.html>

Printed in Poland
by Amazon Fulfillment
Poland Sp. z o.o., Wrocław

20170951R00096